THE DNA OF
AFRICAN DIASPORA

THE BLACK USA

SEBASTIAN JOSEPH

PARTRIDGE

To order additional copies of this book, contact
Partridge India
000 800 919 0634 (Call Free)
+91 000 80091 90634 (Outside India)
orders.india@partridgepublishing.com

www.partridgepublishing.com/india

In this world, there is no other man to replace one man.

Each has its deeds, and it is right to allow those deeds to be done. I submit to you because I have the acts to write this book, and it is not my deeds to hurt anyone personally. I try to share my knowledge through this book based on various sources of knowledge available to me. If you think something is wrong with this message, every African and African diaspora who loves Africa must correct it, filter it, and convey it to African descent. I rest assured that this book will create some influential leaders and entrepreneurs to develop Africa into a better continent. I gladly dedicate this simple book as a humble gift to you.

Racial discrimination is a reality and in the minds of everyone, including me. Intelligent people live decently without exposing it. Some of the foolish have manifested it and hurt even those in his tribe. It is not my intention to offend any nation, color, race, or religion through this book. There is also evidence of what I write based on the knowledge human beings live happily and peacefully in this world.

COLONIAL   -   AFRICA

UNBEARABLE PITY FOR THE SUFFERING OF MANKIND-
Bertrand Russell

I dedicate this book to

All the African leaders and the people of Africa, including
the African diaspora, around the world are dreaming and
working together to build a better African continent, to
fulfill their forefathers' dream of a United States of Africa.
Let the Dark Continent blaze with light
to be a colorful continent.

I Love you all
Sebastian Joseph
Author

- A voice from the spirit of Africa painfully asking.......
- Where are my children now......, who have been snatched away from me for more than five hundred years?
- The evil forces that took my children away from me tore my breast and cut my body into pieces
- The mighty powers of the world show no mercy to my children and me
- They came to my country and wrote on my children's necks a sign saying they were enslaved
- They and their dogs have been sitting where my children should be for a long time
- They are using my children as their weapons to loot my assets
- Some of my children leave the door open for robbers to sacrifice their brothers
- Now, my children are running away to other lands in search of food, and many die in the middle of the sea and by the wayside.
- Generations of those by me centuries ago lived in many countries without knowing me.
- My children, who should be living like kings and queens, are now living as enslaved people
- They took my children hostage, plundered me and all my possessions, and left me to beg in front of others.
- Despite suffering so much and not seeing you for so long, You were not called back for a time when these evil forces were leaving
- All but a few were taken away beyond what they could steal.
- You are the diaspora who can stand up for the rest to throw them away
- As soon as you see this letter, you must return to me with my grandchildren
- I cannot live here without seeing you anymore
- Looking forward to your arrival at the earliest.

With Lots of Love,
Your own 'Mother of Africa'

YOU'RE THINKING ABOUT AFRICA UNTIL TODAY

What image comes to your mind when you think of Africa?

A group of insecure and none developing emerging countries?

Have you ever wondered if you can safely return from Africa if you go to Africa?

The land of thieves and murderers?

Haven't you heard so many?

If this is how you feel in your mind, the advertisement of those who have been looting Africa for more than five hundred years has been successful.

But how many of you know until today that over 60% of the natural resources and precious metals such as Diamond, Gold, Platinum, Silver, Zinc, Lead, Sulphur, Phosphate, Bauxite, Nickel, Copper, Iron, Tantalite, Tin, Uranium, Limestone, Oil & Gas, Coal and many more are exported officially or looted from Africa to Europe, United States, China, United Kingdom, Russia, Asia and more such leading countries?

How many of you know Cocoa, the raw material for most of the chocolate we eat, is 80% produced in Africa?

The real-world global power knows the next potential growth continent with 17% of the world population, 9.6% of global oil output, 90% of world platinum supply, 90% of the world's cobalt supplies, half of the world gold suppliers, two-thirds of the world's manganese, 35% of the world's uranium supplies, 75% of world Cotton supplies and 54 votes in the united nations general assembly is what Africa attractive yet Africa still poor in front of the world and the citizen of Africa still hunger and poverty.

Some 67 million tourists visited Africa in 2018, representing a rise of 7% from a year earlier, making Africa the second-fastest-growing region for tourism after the Asia Pacific. To the best of your knowledge, have you ever heard of these tourists being harassed or killed by any Africans or even African wild animals? This is just one example of who is behind the scandal surrounding Africa.

As you read this book, you will find more evidence that the African continent is feeding on the big countries mentioned above. They probably are starving if African resources are unavailable, say they provide Africa. If you want to change your evil thoughts about Africa, you must visit Africa at least once, and you have come to your decision.

This time for Africa.............. Business opportunities await those who dare to try and start some business in Africa, and many are already doing successfully.

Raise your voice against the countries that plunder Africa and lead Africa into poverty; save Arica and the African people.

CONTENTS

ABOUT THIS BOOK

Note: This book does not condemn any good people; it does not discriminate between black and white or brown, so good people should not be worried regardless of any color; in the meantime, it is a humble request to the wrong people to change to be a better human. Because birth and death are not by our ability, our ability is measured not by how long we lived but by how we lived.

"If you can't live longer, live deeper."

Slavery is the greatest evil and cruelty that humans can do to other human beings. Today, Africa is ruled by a group of people who politicize it and reap the benefits. Those who do not react when they see wrong things are not human. It's more about what you did when you were alive than how long you lived. It has become a habit to react when I see the wrong things. I do not grieve over the dangers of reacting, responding to how long I will live. Before leaving this world, I am now on a journey searching for the deeds assigned to me. I have no right to decide where that journey will end, and I submit it to the Creator of the universe. No limit believe in humanity but not limited to the Continent, Caste, Color, Race, Religion, and love of human beings. Human love has only one language and no boundaries like the ocean.

No matter how much money a person has when he says goodbye to this world, it is transferred from him to another; at the same time, his name does not remain, but his name survives even when he says goodbye to this world as he shares his wealth and wisdom of knowledge with others. We do not have any relatives before we are born, we do not have any relatives when we die, but we get relatives only when we are alive, so make maximum relatives when you are busy.

On this earth, oxygen and light can be shared by big and small, black and white. But water and food have been denied to some people by some devilish attitude group of people. It is the right of every human being to respond and react to this. Because this land does not belong to anyone's family property, it is not to be claimed by a few countries or a few people to rule this land. Some countries automatically seize power and invade and oppress countries that are less capable than they are, and the process intensifies as no one responds. The organs of the human body have every karma, and every human being is entrusted with every karma, so let them fulfill it happily and leave this earth.

This book mainly invites the African diaspora living in different parts of the world whose ancestors were enslaved centuries ago to come to their native motherland of Africa. The desire of some leaders to liberate the African people from colonialism, who have been enslaved for centuries. But some bad African leaders again enslaved the African people to the same colonialists for their interest.

For many centuries many have loved and killed Africa and her children. Probably because of the increased love, they have enslaved you and transplanted you to too many lands? So many of African descent have forgotten Africa and are living in many countries around the world as the diaspora. The invaders who entered Africa practiced racism and were labeled as blacks and portrayed as ugly by that color. Nobody can say that because black and white are human biological orders, white is not superior to black, or black is not inferior to white. Leaders who were supposed to help the African people forgot themselves and became slaves to the food and luxuries of colonial devils.

I wish all of you must listen to this song – *"Imagine" by John Lennon & The Plastic Ono Band* – https://youtu.be/YkgkThdzX-8.

Imagine there's no heaven.
It's easy if you try.
No hell below us
Above us, only the sky

Imagine all the people living today.......

It is the habit of some to find fault with others to cover up their incompetence. Such people keep talking about corruption and the negative news in that country. Those who want to better themselves or want the government to be better off do not make such accusations. They will fight against it, and none of this applies to good leaders and the ness people.

It is not the time to take revenge, nor the time to think wise to build your kingdom, which is the African Kingdom.

COVID WILL MAKE AFRICA RICH - COVID19 Pandemic was made upside down for most countries worldwide. Still, it looks like a blessing to Africa because now all the present African leaders realize that Africa is more significant than any other continent.

"If you want to go fast, go alone. If you want to go far, go together."

With lots of love,
Sebastian Joseph

AFRICA IN BRIEF

"No men should be measured by wealth, color, or sizes because the goodness and knowledge within that man are greater than anything else."

What is history means?

History is not a recollection of events in the past, but rather a recollection of memories flashing through the mind in moments of danger- Walter Benjamin, Philosopher.

We all live on this planet with the accumulated and transformed memories of each of our cells from our generations of ancestors. As far as this land of remembrance is concerned, we are all just pieces of life that need to be stored within our bodies for a very concise and then passed on to the next generation. *"A 21ˢᵗ-century memory sticks with the ability to move and make decisions on your own"*.

On the most significant steps in early human evolution, scientists agree that the 'First human' was discovered in Ethiopia. Scientists have unearthed the jawbone of what they claim is one of the very first humans. The first human ancestors appeared between five million and seven million years ago, probably when some African apelike creatures began to walk habitually on two legs. They were flaking crude stone tools by 2.5 million years ago. Around 1.2 million to 1.8 million years ago, early Homo sapiens evolved dark skin. But evolutionary biologists haven't been convinced that skin cancer drove the evolutionary change.

Homo sapiens or humans evolved in Africa about 200,000 years ago, reaching modernity about 50,000 years ago. Before the arrival of humans in Europe, the Middle East, and Asia, these places were inhabited by another species of hominoid, Homo heidelbergensis or Neanderthals.

In the 21st Century, many people are still living in Africa, much worse than in centuries of the policy of occupiers and greedy nations with the worst colonial mentality. Even in the 21st century, some of the largest countries are still looting the assets of the smallest countries in Africa and its people, just like how the giant whales eat small fish in the oceans. Some of these intellectuals infuse people with caste, religion, and color, fight each other up and find pleasure in drinking their blood.

A child asked Mahatma Gandhi, "What is democracy?"

Mahatma Gandhi replied that when you win a race, democracy is not just about winning; it's also about remembering that some people ran with you.

Again he told me that no one wins if he runs alone.

Next question to Mahatma Gandhi, "What to do with the law?"

Mahatma Gandhi replied that it must be violated; the crowd became violent and asked him, shouldn't the law be obeyed?

He said: The law must be obeyed, and citizens must do so; until the law is fair, Justice is essential, not law.

Yes, the time has come for the African people to receive justice, and African people must wake up now and break the law if there is no justice.

Important note:

"This book is not responsible for any form of argument that the source of human birth is from God or science, and that belief is one of the fundamental rights of every human being, your faith and belief is important to you" moreover, this book gives no value to those who sacrifice their brothers and sisters for the Gods by infiltrating caste and religion without allowing human beings to live as human beings.

ALKEBULAN

"The ancient name of Africa was Alkebulan. Albu-lan **"mother of mankind" or "Garden of Eden."** Alkebulan is the oldest and the only word of indigenous origin. It was used by the Moors, Nubians, Numidians, Khart-Haddans, and Ethiopians.

"Quoted in the Bible and the Qur'an, the Garden of Eden, will it be in Africa?" if so, as per religion, our First Father Adam and First Mother Eve must be born in Africa; if not, as per science, first Human born in Africa. **"So be proud to be an African."**

Nobody can deny the African continent is rich by all means. Africa became poor because of the colonialists in search of the shining treasure of the Black Continent. All the thieves and robbers came and took away the treasures of Africa. It was started more than five hundred years, and it is continued. But the truth is that even though 10% of the wealth is not explored from this most prosperous continent, colonial aggression still exists in Africa.

Between the 1870s and 1900, Africa faced European imperialist aggression, diplomatic pressures, military invasions, and eventual conquest and colonization. At the same time, African societies put up various forms of resistance against the attempt to colonize their countries and impose foreign domination. By the early twentieth century, however, much of Africa, except Ethiopia and Liberia, had been occupied by European powers.

Some animals prey on others to starve, but is the century the need for humans to plunder and kill others and die some? Is this what is needed in this century? This is the humanity you, the colonialists, have taught and are teaching others?

Portuguese, Belgians, British, Germans, France, Italians, Americans, and Spain were the colonizers of Africa. Half a century ago, these invaders ruled without giving any authority or mercy to the African people. But it was only when other countries began to speak out against this slavery that they were willing to back down. Yet many countries still do not shy away from it because once they have tasted it in the meantime. Throughout the 21st century, the direct involvement of some European countries has continued to be brutal in about fourteen countries. Except for some countries in Africa and some humanitarian leaders, no one is raising their voices against it, including African Union, the USA, and United Nations, until today. They aim to proclaim that Africa is to be poor because not to attract other countries over there and not to see the wealth of Africa.

History does not show that so much property and people were plundered from any continent other than Africa.

After World War II in 1945, most European countries became the victims of poverty, hunger, and homelessness. So, they realized that the only easy way to regain wealth was through African minerals and other resources. France has been holding the national reserves of fourteen African countries since 1961: Benin, Burkina Faso, Guinea-Bissau, Ivory Coast, Mali, Niger, Senegal, Togo, Cameroon, Central African Republic, Chad, Congo-Brazzaville, Equatorial Guinea, and Gabon.

From 1880-to 1900, Britain gained control over or occupied what is now known as Egypt, Sudan, Kenya, Uganda, South Africa, Gambia, Sierra Leone, northwestern Somalia, Zimbabwe, Zambia, Botswana, Nigeria, Ghana, and Malawi. That meant that the British ruled 30% of Africa's people at one time.

From 1891 the six principal colonies of German Africa, along with native kingdoms and politics, were the legal precedents for the modern states of Burundi, Cameroon, Namibia, Rwanda, Tanzania, and Togo.

Belgian colonial empire. Belgium controlled two colonies during its history, the Belgian Congo (modern DRC) from 1908 to 1960 and Rwanda-Burundi from 1922 to 1962.

The Portuguese-speaking African countries, also known as Lusophone Africa, consist of six African countries in which the Portuguese language is an official language: Angola, Cape Verde, Guinea-Bissau, Mozambique, São Tomé, and Príncipe.

Italy colonized Libya, Somalia, Eritrea and Ethiopia (Addis Ababa - only for five years), Libya, and Somaliland.

Thus, the single continent of Africa was divided into 54-55 smaller nations, and the occupiers began to divide and rule according to their power. So, they made starve to death the African people and reap the benefits, putting the majority of the African people to fighting against each other. The festival of all European colonists lasted for more than five hundred years and continues with their inexpensive weapons such as religion and viruses. It is one of the most significant colonial agendas until today to reduce the population of Africa by all means so that they can loot the assets from Africa without any problems, for that they are kept on developing various viruses, and it is reached to **OMICRON. You will see the new series of so many in the future.**

Here is the proof: A 1981 book by Bilderberger Jacques Attalli is an example of the Elite Mindset:

"The future will be about finding a way to reduce the population. Of course, we will not be able to execute people to build camps. We get rid of them by making them believe it is for their good… We will find or cause something, a pandemic targeting certain people, a real economic crisis or not, a virus affecting the old or the elderly; it doesn't matter; the weak and the fearful will succumb to it. The stupid will believe in it and ask to be treated. We will have taken care of having panned the treatment, a treatment that will be the solution. Therefore, the selection of idiots will be made by itself: they will go to the slaughterhouse alone."

But we have no choice other than to obey the government rules.

Newton's third law is: **Every action has an equal and opposite reaction. Those working injustice to African people also must be careful about this law.**

You are mistaken if you think the property acquired by cheating on others can live happily for your next generation. It makes you sick so quickly and destroys your offspring that you end up grieving and dying in a nursing home without even getting the love of your children. It can be seen that it is inscribed in many scriptures, and it is true. Because we didn't see the three generations before us, they didn't reserve what many of us enjoy today.

This is a south Indian song, and it is very accurate when you think about Africa;

"Man created religions
Religions created gods
Man, religions, and gods joined
The soil shared; the mind shared
Where is truth? Where is beauty?
where is freedom, where are our blood ties"......... **at the end, he wrote**....
Man dies on the streets. Religions laugh.......

Dr. Arikana Chihombori Quao, Former Permanent Representative of the African Union Mission to the USA, is asking in her speech to the public;

Before giving independence from their 14 colonized countries, France could manage to agree by force as their wish except for two countries which are the Republic of Mali and the Republic of Guinea. Mali and Guinea were not settled to France's demand. As a result, France eradicated these two countries' economies, including the concrete sewage. By knowing this, other countries were forced to sign the agreement to avoid the same consequences waiting for their country from France. Is this the way human rights work? Who had questioned them when they did this evil thing to the suffering countries?

Is there no limit to the shameless exploitation of poor people?

Those countries that agreed to sign the contract must deposit 85% of the asset's income to the French Central bank, and the French Ministry of Finance will control that income. If those countries wish to request their money for domestic use, they must submit the financial statement and wait for their mercy to get back as loan by paying the business loan by commercial interest rate. But because of the various pressure, they reduced from 85% up to 50% but still, they must deposit their income to French Central Bank. This process continued until the 21st Century of June 2020.

Again, she asks, "Why should this poor country give 500 billion dollars annually to France."

Can you imagine depositing all your money and then when you are taking a loan from your own money? Every year France manages to get over 500 billion dollars from these 12 Countries. All this money French Government works collecting the stock market without giving any benefit to those countries, and if they spend for the good of those countries, why do those countries remain poor? France is taking 300 to 500 billion dollars from these countries and telling these countries they are poor. Why the United Nations or any other countries are not taking action against this.....

I'm sorry if I'm wrong, but if my thoughts are correct, can these countries take a good step to correct this mistake and save Africa?

Why are these countries at the top of the list of poor people?

The Central African Republic, Democratic Republic of Congo, Republic of Congo: One of the biggest Cocoa producers in the world other than the Gana and Ivory coast, exporting/looting all over Europe to produce the best chocolates and cocoa products. The place of Diamond, Gold, Copper, and many more....The world's lion shares gold, graphite, ilmenite, iron ore, kaolin, kyanite, lignite, limestone, manganese, monazite, quartz, rutile, salt, tin, and uranium yet these countries. These are the significant minerals for the world's manufacturing requirements. These minerals are mined and exported legally or illegally in these countries, yet why are they in poverty and hunger. UN Military presence there for very long years. Are these UN troops protecting the people or the thieves?

France is the colonizer and the permanent among five Veto power members country in United Nations; China is colonizing with their money and extracting all the raw material to their country for their manufacturing factories from Arica. The United Kingdom was the biggest colonizer worldwide, and Russia and the United States of America were the most significant manufacturers in the world. What mercy can you expect from these Veto Power countries to the United Nations for Africa? The latest update now Israel also started their political agenda in Africa. If Africa is poor, why are all these superpower countries in Africa? What for? Why does Africa remain poor if these countries protect Africa and its people?

"The above-said countries are controlling the United Nations Pease keep force and talking more about human rights. Isn't this the equivalent of giving a key to a thief?"

We should not forget that no African country was independent at the time of the formation of the United Nations Organization. Remember again that the two countries, France and the United Kingdom, were the colonizers of Africa and the present VETO power country. **"Therefore, the United Nations needs to revise this decision, as it was made without African countries and some other countries were under colonization, including India"** This world is not the homeland of only five countries to control. What do other leaders in this world fear in their own lives?

All human beings have the same right to live on this earth, and the natural resources of one country may not be available in other countries so that they can share with other nations and buy their share from them, but not by encroachment. If it had done so, how much richer would the continent of Africa have been if it had given Africa 10% of what was mined in Africa for more than five hundred years and exported to other countries? May this decision not be delayed any longer, and the African people live decently in front of others in the coming years.

What is the role of the United Nations in the World? Here we go;

The UN was established after World War II to prevent future wars. The United Nations (UN) is an intergovernmental organization that aims to maintain international peace and security, develop friendly relations among nations, achieve international cooperation, and be a center for harmonizing the actions of governments. **"But now it works opposite"** How many countries are peaceful because of the UN agenda in the Middle East and Africa until today?

The UN is headquartered on international territory in New York City. World peace, or peace on Earth, is the concept of an ideal state of happiness, freedom, and peace within and among all people and nations on Planet Earth.

"How many countries are in peace other than Europe?

Syria, Lydia, Egypt, Iran, Iraq, Yemen, South Sudan, Central African Republic, Republic of Congo, Mozambique, and many more are in peace?" whichever countries will find high-value natural resources in their countries, such as Oil and Gas and precious mineral will be in trouble for sure.** Therefore, the United Nations-ruled countries have set aside these resources for certain countries; others must fight and die in the name of caste, color, religion, and GOD, which is true.

Since 1945, the United Nations and the five permanent members of its Security Council **(China, France, Russia, the United Kingdom, and the United States)** have operated to resolve conflicts without war or declarations of war. The time has come for all nations to rewrite the current laws of the United Nations. Or it is time to form another United Nations to compete with the present United Nations.

Rules are subject to change over time; please rewrite all laws for the betterment of all people worldwide; this is a humble request. Many leaders and scriptures have taught us that we can achieve much not only through violence but also through love.

CHAPTER - 2

MY NEXT TOUR TO AFRICA

"If you want something, the whole universe will conspire to help you" By PAULO COELHO.

Africa has a natural beauty that no other continent can claim except a few. The important thing is that you want to get there..... One's mission is to strive for this desire.

- **Snow-capped mountains,**
- **tree-lined hills,**
- **streams flowing from the mountains,**
- **serene blue lakes,**
- **the rhythmic oceans of the earth,**
- **birds singing to the rhythm of the morning until evening,**
- **The embracing blue and White Nile River that flows through entire Africa,**
- **The river Congolese, which flows uncontrollably with its total current**
- **Large and small animals and birds migrate from one country to another without a passport or visa, depending on climate change.**
- **Dense forests and small and large animals are adorning the forest. On which continent can you see altogether?**

- **Africa is a dazzling storehouse of wonders with unique treasures.**

If you do not go to Africa before you leave this earth, it will be a significant loss, especially to the African Americans and the diaspora around the world.

What you presently know about the American or European media is not true about Africa; they make you scared by all means not looking into Africa. When you reach Africa, you can see the same as the National Geographic Chanel videos live in front of you. The souls of your ancestors are waiting for your arrival; you feel it when you set foot on that soil. Then you will unknowingly ask yourself, **"why am I so late to come here"?**

The best way to know about your motherland is to go for a tour of Africa first. Then you will tell the world that the news you hear is not the truth about Africa. If you go to Africa, you cannot see the fake shows on the European channels. You are visualizing or listening to the UnitedNations' fake dramas. History shows some of the present permanent VETO power members are the colonialist of Africa. Or the current weapon manufacturers or suppliers to Africa want to show the world that Africa is poor and unrestrained. They plan to not look into that continent, for they spend millions only on advertising to show that Africa is poor and unrest. Yes, the people are still lacking because of white colonialism.

Why is this African tour essential for African Diaspora?

The young generation of the African Diaspora may not know who they are and where they came from. The children of Africa even may not know what Africa is. The young generation must understand that the bad news and propaganda you hear is false. This is fabricated intentionally to show the world that Africa is poor and always unrest. The colonialists plan to make that country unrest to loot the valuable minerals like Gold, Copper, Uranium, Cobalt, Diamond, etc. The raw material Tantalum (tantalum capacitor is widely used in communications, aerospace and military industries, submarine cables, advanced electronic devices, civil appliances, televisions, and many other aspects) mobile phone and another type of batters are going from Central Africa, Republic of Congo, Rwanda, Namibia and many more.....

Until now, you can see in the Central African Republic the soldiers parade with artillery weapons marching to the local street to show that we are present here to show the people; even the children also know it is a drama because they are seeing even from the time they born. You can see the Pakistan Army from the peacekeeping force in these countries. The children are smiling and running along with them while they pass their parade in the street.

To know the absolute truth, you must visit Africa at the earliest. But remember, you may not see the five-star hotels or seven-star facilities because Africa was under the colonialists for five centuries. Their job was not to develop or help Africa.

Their only aim is to loot the raw materials and precious metals to exploit and steal from Africa for their own countries' benefit. Yes, now in some developing countries in Africa you can see and enjoy the five-star facilities. **You can see one of the best cleanest African cities in Kigali, Rwanda.** It would help if you remembered that you might not need these facilities once you land in Africa. The natural organic food and the light breeze that caresses your mind and body are enough to replace all other luxuries. It will be a fantastic feeling and natural meditation from Africa's weather.

Fantastic Tourist Destination in Africa.

Kenya - Kenya is a country in East Africa with a coastline on the Indian Ocean. It's also home to wildlife like lions, elephants, and rhinos. From Nairobi, the capital, safaris visit the Maasai Mara Reserve, known for its annual wildebeest migrations, and Amboseli National Park, offering views of Tanzania's 5,895m Mt. Kilimanjaro. Mount Kilimanjaro National Park will take you to your dream paradise.

Over 25 National parks, over 20 National Reserves, over five marine parks and reserves, Team farms, all kinds of agricultural farms, and many more you can visit and see the animals you have seen on

National Geographic channels. In some of the parks, you can touch the wild animals, which will be a fun, thrilling moment in your life.

Tanzania – Tanzania is an East African country known for its vast wilderness areas. Tanzania is worth a country to Visit all months yearly. Plenty of Wildlife and animal spots, and each National point, as per the itinerary indicated, has its uniqueness and self-sole of enjoyment tour. They include the plains of Serengeti National Park, a safari mecca populated by the elephant, lion, leopard, buffalo, rhino, and Kilimanjaro National Park, home to Africa's highest mountain. Offshore lie the tropical islands of Zanzibar, with Arabic influences, with a marine park home to whale sharks and coral reefs.

Zanzibar Island is a must-visit place; Stone Town gets its name from the ornate houses built with local stone by Arab traders and slavers during the 19th Century. It is estimated that around 600,000 enslaved people were sold through Zanzibar between 1830-1863. In 1822, the British signed the first of a series of treaties with Sultan Said to curb this trade, but not until 1876 was the sale of enslaved people finally prohibited. Under intense British pressure, the slave trade was officially abolished in 1876, but slavery remained legal in Zanzibar until 1897. Maybe some of your ancestors reached America from this trade?????

Botswana – Botswana, a landlocked country in Southern Africa, has a landscape defined by the Kalahari Desert and the Okavango Delta, which becomes a lush animal habitat during the seasonal floods. The massive Central Kalahari Game Reserve, with its fossilized river valleys and undulating grasslands, is home to numerous animals, including giraffes, cheetahs, hyenas, and wild dogs. This is the place of the world's most prosperous diamond mining. The well-organized government systems for tourism will take you to the tourist places with the world's best Beef meat dishes around Botswana.

Ethiopia – Ethiopia, the Horn of Africa. According to history, this is the only country in Africa that surrendered to Italy to colonize for only five years, that too only in the capital, Addis Ababa. Ethiopia is a rugged, landlocked country split by the Great Rift Valley. With archaeological finds dating back more than 3 million years, it's a place of ancient culture. Among the important sites in Lalibela with its rock-cut Christian churches from the 12th–13th centuries. Aksum is the ruins of an ancient city with obelisks, tombs, castles, and Our Lady Mary of Zion church. The hospitality and entertainment will take your soul to heaven.

Zimbabwe – Zimbabwe is a landlocked country in southern Africa known for its dramatic landscape and diverse wildlife, much of it within parks, reserves, and safari areas. On the Zambezi River, Victoria Falls make a thundering 108m drop into narrow Batoka Gorge, where there's white-water rafting and bungee-jumping. Matusadona and Mana Pools national parks are downstream, home to hippos, rhinos, and birdlife.

Egypt - Egypt, a country linking northeast Africa with the Middle East, dates to the time of the pharaohs. This country, which was rich two thousand years ago, has a great place in the Bible. Many of Egypt's architecture is impressive, despite some political issues. Millennia-old monuments sit along the fertile Nile River Valley, including Giza's colossal Pyramids and Great Sphinx, Luxor's hieroglyph-lined Karnak Temple, and Valley of the King's tombs. The capital, Cairo, is home to Ottoman landmarks like the Muhammad Ali Mosque and the Egyptian Museum, a trove of antiquities.

Namibia - Namibia, a country in southwest Africa, is distinguished by the Namib Desert along its Atlantic Ocean coast. The government is home to diverse wildlife, including a significant cheetah population. The capital, Windhoek, and coastal town Swakopmund contain German colonial-era buildings such as Windhoek's Christuskirche, built-in 1907. Etosha National Park's salt pan draws games in the north, including rhinos and giraffes.

And many more....

Tourism Business Opportunity for American and European Diaspora

Few countries are still in trouble; among 55 African countries in the African Continent controlled by the colonials from their back office with the support of the wrong political leaders are still in danger. Especially the francophone African countries. In these countries, people are under fear and starvation. The weapon blasting sounds have become customary for these people. Because even if there are no problems, they will ensure the people are under surveillance of the colonial thief. These are the countries the peacekeeping forces controlling for over 40 years; controlling means supporting the mineral looters' protection, and the only job they are doing is throwing a few sacks of food and medicine from the United Nations Fund. That's all.

In all other countries you can travel to without any problems, the local people and government will assist you without need. They welcome tourists to their countries to come and see how Africa is now.

These African country leaders are expecting your investment contribution to developing their country. Over 35 Countries are safe, and the diaspora can think of opening Tourist Hotels up to 5 Stars and resorts. The diaspora from America and Europe and arrange the tour package to Africa.

Millions of tourists from Asia, the Middle East, the Far East, America, Australia, and Europe visit annually. So, no security problems were reported for the tourists. Building Five Star Hotels and resorts will be much cheaper than in the USA and Europe. The availability of raw materials and labor costs will reduce the capital investment. Also, to operate the Hotels, you can find educated, humble African people with less salary payment.

It will be a great business opportunity for the American diaspora and the present tourist visiting Africa. The current tourists coming to Africa demand more facilities and are ready to spend the money for the facilities. All the other continents are struggling for job opportunities, and a million people lost their job because of the present pandemic of COVID19. But Africa faced challenges more significant than these diseases and pandemics. Even now, the less COVID19 less affected area and less death reported are only in the African continent. *Remember, if the vaccine has made before the pandemic like all other viruses by the drug mafia, then it was supposed to be a different story; you may see that Africa will be the first victim of COVID19 like any other virus.* Because they test the drug on the animals first, and after that, they will inject it into Africans. But I am sure these colonial's plan was to proclaim that Africa is a dangerous place so that we may see the new variant of Virus-like Omicron or Demicron and many other Crones. All the 26 alphabets in the English letter Corn Viruses will be tested in Africa. They are killing millions of innocent people through viruses to make money for a few.

The African Free Trade

The 2018 African Free Trade Agreement will bring up the economy in Africa in a different style. The dream of the African forefathers - Kwame Nkrumah of Ghana, Haile Selassie of Ethiopia, Kenneth Kaunda of Zimbabwe, Ahmadu Ibrahim Bello of Nigeria, Uhuru Muigai Kenyatta of Kenya, Julius Kambarage Nyerere of Tanzania, Thomas Isidore Noël Sankara of Burkina Faso, Apollo Milton Obote of Uganda and other leaders dream was to build **United States of Africa** (Another USA in Africa) to bring as one nation and one military power so that nobody can beat African continent in terms of resources and workforce.

Unfortunately, the colonialists implemented their plan to divide and rule during the Berlin Conference conducted in Congo from November 15, 1884 – to February 26, 1885. The colonialists set this bad policy to prevent the African generation from moving from one country to another. (Until now, the fact is that any of the African Countries does not control the Air Space). The Berlin Conference favored only the colonialists, not the African people. This helped to stop the colonialists from fighting each other inside the African continent and controlling their occupied territories. In this Belin conference meeting, the truth was the colonialists decided, and they shared each African state and set the boundaries among themselves according to their colonial occupational power. But African leaders and the people of Africa believed that this meeting was for Africa's betterment.

It was impossible for the free movement of goods and the people of Africa if the African Free Trade Agreement was not signed in 2018 and for the tourist to go from one country to another. The African Continental Free Trade Area includes 28 countries. The African Continental Free Trade Agreement created it among 54 of the 55 African Union nations. This will help the same as the tourists traveling to Europe with Schengen Tourist Visa.

Imagine if the tour companies started their branches in each African country with agricultural farms, food manufacturing processing, Tourist Resorts, restaurants, Bars, Dance Clubs, Safaris, Tourist transport, etc. No other countries in this 21st century have the opportunity like Africa. This is what the tourists are looking for. You don't need to bring any materials to start with other than a few electronics items. All are available in Africa now.

Let Kanye West's footwear and apparel brand, "Yeezy," be produced in 54 African countries, and all the African children use these shoes on the African Streets. Let his disaster relief fund use the African minority Children around the African continent.

Let Jay-Z's entertainment network, dress collection, and Shawn Carter Foundation serve the African people and the entire African Continent of 54 countries.

Let Sheela Johnson's Hotels, Resorts, and Spa open with 54 Countries in Africa to entertain and serve the tourist coming to Africa from America and around the world.

Let Diddy's entertainment Chanel and film production, Clothing lines, Fragrance, Wine and spirit, etc., open to entertaining the 54 Countries in Africa. Let his charity foundation serve Africa as well.

Let Tiger Woods' Golf Court and Restaurant Open in 54 African countries. So, the African Tourists people can enjoy their tour, and the African people will get the job opportunity.

So, Africa is going to be a paradise for tourists. Remember, this is your own country; your American Passports are valid in Africa and protect the local people.

"Everyone can be the best in the world for something."

Manufacturing Opportunity in Africa:

"African ground is ready to start the league game. All other teams are already practicing in the African ground, Chinese, American, Europeans, and Asian **but only the African diaspora team is missing in the African ground."**

African diaspora,

- Are you more incompetent and inferior than the Chinese, Europeans, Asians, or other countries?
- Are you afraid of going to your own country to build your own business?
- All the contracts are going to Chinese and European companies;

It is not the African leaders or Chinese fault because you are not on the ground to play the game. You are not biding off any of the tenders, or you are not coming like the Chinese with their little investments together into one basket and minding millions from African countries. If you as a diaspora go with your investment, all African leaders will treat you like kings and queens and would like to award the tender without asking anyone.

When the Chinese get the contract, they bring professionals and educated people from their own country. They gave challenging labor job opportunities to African people only for the labor class and then again treated them as enslaved. *In effect, Africans are still not escaped from slavery even in the 21st Century.* It is only because of the absence of the African diaspora.

To start manufacturing in Africa, you must procure only the technology from any other country. All other resources such as raw material- you name it, it is available in the African continent, infrastructure (If not, you build yourself. That is another opportunity), and a highly-skilled workforce that you don't need to export from any other continent than Africa. Because so far, Africa does not produce what Africa consumed. The 55 small African countries eagerly await your production for their consumption. Very soon, all these 55 African Countries will convert into 55 states as one country in the African continent without losing their leader's power; that was the forefather's dream of the **United States of Africa-USA.**

This message to the African diaspora businessmen and women doing business around the world, if you believe that your DNA is from Africa, it is your moral responsibility to open a business in Africa to support African children who are highly educated with Engineering and Master's degrees, they only need the people like you to show their ability to prove that African children can do better than anybody else. Your Billions and Millions of dollars showing in the bank account are just paper statements if you are not using them for a good purpose. Go back to two generations of history and check the records of the millionaires. How many of them are remembered in this generation? Maybe one or two percentages; what is the use of that money? Do you think the next generation will enjoy it peacefully? Probably not. The current record shows many children are addicted to heavy-dose drugs, which have spoiled their life. Some of their children are in retreat centers in India or other countries, looking for harmony in their minds. Today we see more and more children ruined by the misdeeds of their rogue parents.

Those names will be remembered if they have done something for society and the poor. Those names will be remembered forever in the history book with the golden letters. That is their signature to the world before they leave the earth. Those millionaires must understand that you may have a small rich circle of influence on several people, and you now think that is the absolute joy. It's not because that may not be the real love. If you want to see real love from the heart, you must go to Africa and support the poor people to improve their lives. So, you will see thousands of people talking about you with great passion and love; your billions or millions cannot tally with that love. *The definition of "Business" means to make someone's life better. That includes you and the people around you.*

Recently Professor PLO Lumumba asked a question about the wrong political leaders. You are stealing millions and billions of dollars from each country; what will you do with that money? Other than sending this money to the USA, Europe, Swiss Account, British Virgin Island, or some other hidden islands? They welcome this kind of investors and their investments because their blood is also looted from somewhere. Does it not mean you again give African money to the same colonizer's hand and turn your brothers and sisters into hunger and poverty?

Wow... What a helpful question! If those leaders feel at least one percent of shame within themselves, they will suicide the next moment. Do you think putting the dog's tail into the straight pipe for a long time... will it change? You cannot expect not more from those people.

As an African, you need food and enjoyment; a million dollars will be sufficient for your two or three generations. The moment they pump their looted money to another country, their days are counted in the graveyard. From that day onwards, mental harmony will be destroyed by that looted money, leading to a high level of illness. Thanks to the Hi-Fi European and American super-specialty hospitals, you will treat these bad political leaders by compensating for their looted money. An average farmer can sleep better than that bad political leader in harmony. Did you enjoy eating and sleeping together as a family today? (No matter what you eat and how you sleep) Then rejoice because you are rich today. Because some of those rich people have millions and billions in their banks. **They have silk mattresses but can't sleep, Five Star meals but can't eat, a husband and wife cannot sleep together, there are children and privileges, but there is no peace. So, what is the point of over-appropriating excess wealth?**

Life is not all about making millions or billions of monies. Imagine this- you have your wishes which are a lot of money, a good house, good cars, the food you prefer every day and the other enjoyment you wish and now you have received everything in front of you. What will you need again... a peaceful mind, yes?

Do you think that looted money can make that peaceful mind harmonized?

Hallow???? Are you there????

REMEMBER, IF YOU DON'T GO TO AFRICA AND PUT BUSINESS AS YOUR SIGNATURE NOW, THEN FORGET AFRICA FOREVER.

CHAPTER 3

BE PROUD TO BE AN AFRICAN

Arikana Chihombori-Quao – Former African Union Ambassador to the United States. This beautiful Mother (All the African people wish to call her Mama) is a medical doctor and activist. She is a public speaker, educator, diplomat, and entrepreneur. She moved to the United States after living many years in Zimbabwe. She is the CEO and founder of Bell Family Medical Centers in the United States. This Mama can teach, educate and motivate all the diaspora worldwide. This mother's ability to proclaim the truth without fear is immense.

African descent diaspora can play a significant role in saving and making Africa rich. For that, you have to believe Africa is your mother country; you should be proud that you are an African by forgetting your race, color, and inferiority complex. You are black because your father is black and your mother is a good woman; therefore, you are born black. To love Africa, you have to believe in yourself. Only then will you have a passion for loving Africa. By the way, we must not forget that not all Africans are black. Whatever the color, it is enough if the mind is white.

Because of various circumstances, you are now living in some other parts of the world as a diaspora, and it is not your fault. You may have a green card, permanent residence card, or even citizenship; that does not mean forgetting your own country. Whichever country you live in, your body and mind will be asking for the food from where you were born.

- Don't you feel the urge to enjoy that food from your own country?
- Don't you want to go and play with your children or grandchildren in the playground where you played with your friends when you were young?
- Don't you feel free to relax again in the river where you swam, the hills, and the trees you climbed?
- Have you not felt that the next generation should not be denied the essentials you did not get in the school where you studied?
- If you want to relive those sweet memories before you die, you must make your trip to your homeland of Africa better.

Your best choice is to go to https://ouraddi.org/ The African Diaspora Development Institute and register to support a better Africa.

The African Diaspora Development Institute

Founder: Her Excellency, Ambassador Arikana Chihombori-Quao, MD

The African Diaspora Development Institute (The ADDI) is an entity that was born out of the realization that there is no one-stop-shop for everything African. Business Communities around the world, African Diaspora, or people interested in African tourism must visit 55 African countries to learn about Africa. There's a need for a one-stop organization where people can go to get information about Africa.

There were 37,144,530 non-Hispanic blacks, which comprised 12.1% of the population. This number increased to 42 million according to the 2010 United States Census, including Multiracial African Americans, making up 14% of the total U.S. population.

America is one of the wealthiest countries in the world. Still, according to the Annual Homeless Assessment Report presented to Congress, an estimated 568,000 people experienced homelessness in a single night in the United States in 2019.

This report provides a state-by-state breakdown of unemployment rates by race and ethnicity and racial/ethnic unemployment rate gaps for the fourth quarter of 2018. While there have been state-by-state improvements in prospects for black and Hispanic workers, their unemployment rates remain high relative to those of white workers. More than 8.5 million African Americans are at the poverty line.

Enslaved African's arrival in the USA

Throughout the 17th and 18th centuries, people were kidnapped from the continent of Africa, forced into slavery in the American colonies, and exploited to work as indentured servants and labor in the production of crops such as tobacco and cotton. Though it is impossible to give accurate figures, some historians have estimated that 6 to 7 million enslaved people were imported to the New World during the 18th century alone, depriving the African continent of some of its healthiest and ablest men and women. In addition, historical records show that it was traded to Persian countries such as Iran and Iraq, as well as to Asian countries.

During the same period, healthy young men were trafficked to the United States. Beautiful and healthy black women were trafficked from all over Africa, trading through the port of Tanganyika (Tanzania), Ghana (In 1957, when the leaders of the former British colony of the Gold Coast sought an appropriate name for their newly independent state—the first black African nation to gain its independence from colonial rule—they named their new country after ancient Ghana), South Africa (Zuid-Afrikaanse Republiek or ZAR) to other Arab countries via Oman, and to America and Europe or Asia and elsewhere. Many were used for the sexual needs or domestic work of the capitalist who bought these enslaved women. Some women from this slave trade are lucky because some Arab people took these slave women as their life partners. During that time, the historical records show that such a law existed in the Arab world that an enslaved woman got the child from the owner through his sexual intervention. That child will be free from slavery and become the owner's child, and if that owner passes away, then that woman is also free from slavery. From now onwards, no one can purchase these women as enslaved people.

A Royal Revelation......(AMERICAN DNA FOUND IN AFRICA)

Credit: Martha Asencio Rhine/Tampa Bay Times/Zuma Press
And www.readersdigest.in/features/story-reunited-by-science-a-royal-revelation-127157
Published Apr 5, 2021

Millions of people have used commercial DNA tests to trace their family trees. The results have been life-changing for a few lucky folks, introducing them to relatives they had lost long ago—or never knew existed. This is one of them.

As a descendant of enslaved people, Jay Speights had struggled to find written documentation of his family history. He spent years looking, as his father had before him, but he was 64 before a DNA test offered a solid lead. The pastor from Rockville, Maryland, learned that 30 percent of his DNA was from Benin, a country located to the west of Nigeria, about which Jay knew next to nothing.

At the urging of a friend, he turned to a database called GED Match, which has had success connecting African Americans and their African relatives, to learn more about his link to Benin. After uploading his data to the site, Jay saw a surprising DNA match. The website listed a man named Houanlokonon Deka as his distant cousin. Next to the listing were the words 'royal DNA'. *Beninese royalty?* Jay was stunned. He had no idea what to do next.

But fate—or maybe even divine intervention—kicked in a few months after Jay learned of his royal lineage. At the New Seminary in New York, he met the leader of the West African religion Vodun, who had traveled from his home—in Benin. Jay told the man and his group his unusual story, and one of the Beninese men immediately replied, "I know your king. Here is his number."

"I mean, how could that possibly happen?" Jay says. "After all these years of going through my father's search, going through files ... it just fell in my lap. That's the hand of God."

The first time Jay called King Kpodegbe Toyi Djigla, the traditional ruler of the kingdom of Allada in southern Benin, the king hung up. The second time, the king handed the phone to his English-speaking wife, Queen Djehami Kpodegbe Kwin-Epo. She and Jay started messaging each other online. She told him he was a descendant of King Deka, who had ruled Allada centuries earlier. "We would be delighted to welcome you to your home, dear prince," she wrote.

And so Jay went. On 6 January 2019, his late father's birthday, he landed in Benin. Posters wrote in French, the country's official language, greeted him: "Welcome to the kingdom of Allada, land of your ancestors." At least 300 people were waiting for him outside the airport. They danced, sang, and played instruments to celebrate the return of their long-lost prince.

Accompanied by a motorcade, the queen picked him up from the airport, introduced him to local dignitaries, and showed him some historical sites. When they arrived at the palace for an audience with the king, at least 1,000 people were waiting for them. Jay was overwhelmed with emotion. "I started looking at faces and features. I'm looking for a physical connection to our DNA. Just taking it in," he says. "You're almost dazed because you find yourself in a situation that most African Americans believe you can never step into, that can never happen, and that's to locate the part of your DNA that comes from Africa.

Once Jay composed himself and got out of the car, people cheered and chanted his name. He smiled and waved while walking through the crowd. When he and his interpreter reached the palace, he received a quick lesson in royal etiquette—what he should do when the king entered and how to address Beninese royalty. In the throne room, the king welcomed Jay home, and they spoke about his trip through their interpreters. Later that night, Jay participated in a ritual to show whether his ancestors would accept him into the family. (Luckily, they did.)

How Jay's royal ancestors came to America from Africa remains a mystery. Benin was once home to one of West Africa's biggest slave ports. African royalty would sell war captives into slavery, and some would allow royal family members to travel with European merchants to the New World, where they would usually end up being enslaved. Jay's Beninese relatives told him the royal family of Allada would not have sold their people into slavery, but they couldn't tell him how his ancestors had ended up on a slave ship. He is still grappling with being a descendant of enslaved people and people who led others into slavery, but that knowledge doesn't keep him from embracing his Beninese heritage.

"I've stepped into my identity," he says. "I can point to a place on the map and say, 'The Speights family comes from here, right here.' We're a royal family. We have a history."

Jay has continued to deepen his connection to his homeland. When they met, the king gave him 'princely duties': Once he got back to Maryland, he was to look for ways to bring clean water to the village surrounding the palace in Allada and to promote the kingdom in the United States. Now Jay is partnering with the Rotary Club of Alexandria West in Alexandria, Virginia, to raise money to build wells in the village.

He also searches for others who have DNA from Allada (primarily through GED Match) and introduces them to their ancestral home. After all, not everyone can be lucky enough to be handed the king's phone number.

"In that case, there is no need for further evidence that African DNA has spread to America, Europe, Arab, Persian and Asian countries."

Now the time has come, the African Americans and the diaspora worldwide can shout out loud that I am an African, that my hometown is flowing with honey and milk, and that my DNA is in Africa with pride.

Just as the people of Israel, who lost their homeland for more than five centuries and wandered as strangers and enslaved people, regained their homeland. As a result of their united efforts, the tiny nation of Israel is now rich and powerful. Less than 20 percent of the urban land without freshwater turns into over 60 percent, resulting in Israel being the food basket of their own country and many other countries. Now Israel shares their farming technology with over 110 countries without hiding its self-developed farming techniques. Because of their unity, they now control the latest technologies and the world with their fingertip. So, the nation of Israel, scattered over the world, gathered together when they had a chance.

Unfortunately, in Africa and some other countries priority is to make GOD's life better and save GOD by fighting and killing each other. Their focus is to spread the religion through breaking all the laws of GOD to the people. "Who are you to protect GOD" God had given the direction to make human life better; GOD does not require your support or assistance to save himself. Save yourself and your family by looking into the fertile land, farm yourself to feed your family, and thank God for making GOD happy. Please don't fall into the trap of a group of real business people throwing a dangerous religious weapon at you for their political benefit to reap the gift from you. Remember, if you believe in GOD, then GOD is concerned about only your soul; if you think that we are the creation of GOD, then all the people on the earth are the same creation of GOD; if you believe that soul is in your heart or mind then our body is a Temple, Church or Mosque. Will you destroy your temple, Church or Mosque? If the answer is no, how can you fight and kill each other of GOD's creation? Therefore, don't be a victim of a religious weapon that will not benefit your life. At the same time, you live on this earth until you die because nobody can take this piece of body to heaven or hell regardless of any religion you belong to.

The next turn is for Africa.

This was missing for the African diaspora within America and around the world, the unity. This is the time to think of rebuilding your kingdom, which is the African kingdom—some of the evil forces that enslaved your forefathers and mothers are still playing the same game in Africa. If you want to change the tears of their soul, you, their descendants, must go back to Africa. It was not possible even before 20 years. But now you have the great leaders, especially all Africans affectionately call Mama **Arikana Chihombori-Quao. Many** other leaders will accompany and guide you to reach Africa to fulfill that dream.

Two thousand years ago, from in the desert, that day a voice rose "Bible-Isaiah 1:11 The Multitude of your sacrifices, what is that to me, says the Lord? I am full; I do not desire holocausts of rams, the fat of fatling, or the blood of calves and lambs and he-goats. 1:12 When you approach before my sight, who is it that requires these things from your hands so that you would walk in my courts. 1:13 You should no longer offer sacrifice in vain. Incense is an abomination to me. I will not receive the new moons, the Sabbaths, and the other feast days I will not receive. Your gathering is iniquitous. 1:14 My soul hates your days of proclamation and your solemnities. They have become bothersome to me. I labor to endure them. 1:15 And so, when you extend your hands, I will avert my eyes from you. And when you multiply your prayers, I will not need you. For your hand are full of blood. 1:16 Wash, become clean, take away the evil of your intentions from my eyes. Cease to act perversely".

In the 21st century, another voice shouting out loud from Africa to change the present mentality of Africans, Bishop Joshua Maponga.

Bishop Joshua Maponga takes an in-depth philosophical yet practical approach to ten guiding values: privacy, effort, development, action, self-esteem, sympathy, situations, service, joy, and direction. He offers insight into each deal, how society has corrupted it, and how you can use it to recover and succeed in your life with relationships and business.

Somewhere as aliens who lost everything,

African diaspora that 400 years before your forefathers and mothers were enslaved from some of the areas of the African continent. Most enslaved African people were captured in wars or surprise raids in villages. Adults were bound and gagged, and infants were sometimes thrown into sacks. The arrival of the first captives to the Jamestown Colony in 1619 is often seen as the beginning of slavery in America—but enslaved Africans arrived in North America as early as the 1500s. Tens of thousands of people were forcibly baptized. They lost their parents/children, their names, culture, ethnicity, and Africa from that day onwards.

Bishop Maponga Joshua reminds the African diaspora must return to Africa; they are free to come back to Africa if they want to return. The black Americans were taken from Africa to America without passports; he recommended that black Americans must come back to Africa without visas. They must come back to their forefather's land the same way they went and touch the continent with no names, we have the indigenous way of naming people and finding their cultures, tracing their roots leading, and we have the spiritual technology that can assist people in doing that. Come and stand at the shores of the Atlantic with no name and let the process will do the healing process.

Asserting that "how you believe is how you behave," Maponga shows you that faith- no matter what religion you follow- directly impacts your morality and ability to deal ethically and effectively with current issues.

If you want your work to be fruitful, you must increase your trust in those who lead you.

Many leaders heard the same voice in the voice of Pan-Africanism to bring African descent to unite together. Pan-Africanism is a worldwide movement that aims to encourage and strengthen bonds of solidarity between all indigenous and diaspora ethnic groups of African descent. This idea began in the mid-19th century in the United States of America.

The earliest Pan Africanists or The Saints of Africa

- "Martin Robinson Delany" was an African-American abolitionist, journalist, physician, soldier, and writer, and arguably the first proponent of Black Nationalism. Delany is credited with the Pan-African slogan of **"Africa for Africans.**

- "Edward Wilmot Blyden" was primarily an educator, writer, diplomat, and politician in Liberia. Born in the West Indies, he joined the free black immigrants from the United States who migrated to the region. He taught for five years in the British West African Colony of Sierra Leone in the early 20th century.

- "Marcus Mosiah Garvey Jr. ONH" was a Jamaican political activist, publisher, journalist, entrepreneur, and orator. He was the founder and first President-General of the Universal Negro Improvement Association and African Communities League, through which he declared himself Provisional President of Africa. Garvey, the champion after world War-I, was the cause of African Independence. His organization "UNIA" was gathering millions of Black African Americans envisioning returning Africa Gravy's black star line, a shipping company established to transport black people to Africa and facilitate black global commerce. Unfortunately, this attempt was unsuccessful.

- "Jomo Kenyatta" was an important figure of Pan Africanist and Kenyan anti-colonial activist and politician. He governed Kenya as its Prime Minister from 1963 to 1964 and then its first President from 1964 to his death in 1978.

- "Kwame Nkrumah" was a Ghanaian politician and revolutionary. In the 1950s, Kwame believed European colonialism could extinguish if African leaders united, leading to the first African Independence movement. As a result, Ghana becomes the first independent country in Africa. He was the first Prime Minister and President of Ghana, leading the Gold Coast to independence from Britain in 1957. Followed by many other leaders.

Now the soul of Kwame Nkrumah talks through her daughter's voice, "Samia Yaba Christina Nkrumah," about Pan Africanism. She is a Ghanaian politician and chairperson of the Convention People's Party. In the 2008 parliamentary election, she won the Jomoro constituency seat in her first attempt. She is the daughter of Kwame Nkrumah, the first President of Ghana.

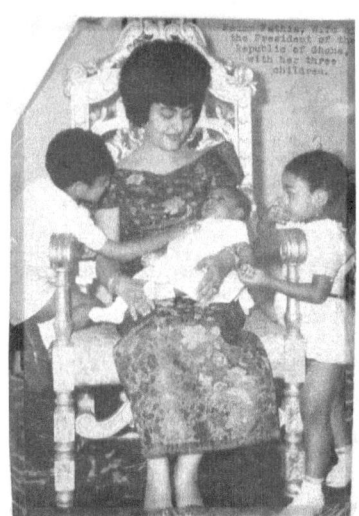

BOLD AND BEAUTIFUL – KWAME NKRUMAH AND FAMILY

When many of today's leaders plunder their own country's assets and smuggle them to other countries, Samia proudly remembers its father, Kwame Nkrumah. He built a house on the land donated by the government to Kwame and dedicated it to the country as his statehouse. He later presented it back to Ghana as its own state house, now the Presidential retreat place "The Pidwasi Lodge" in Abri Hill, Ghana, where she was born. She says that is one of the great lessons inherited from her father. Samia never demands Kwame Nkrumah be not only her father but the Father of all African people without jealousy. Samia Nkrumah calling all the African diaspora says it is the time to fight not physically but mentally to complete the Pan Africanist forefather's dream of the **United States of Africa.**

A man was promised riches if he could swim three kilometers; he swam one and a half kilometers, got tired, and swam back. It takes the same energy to retreat, so invest it in completion.

SO NEVER GIVE UP

CHAPTER - 4

BLACK BILLIONAIRES IN AMERICA

The African leaders and the visionaries of Africa, with the support of Mama Arikana Chihombori-Quao – Former African Union Ambassador to the United States, must meet these American billionaires and open all the way to bring their business to suitable African countries.

Maybe they do not think you are their brothers and sisters; it is the responsibility to open the smooth way and the infrastructure of all the African leaders to bring their investment to Africa. For that, all the leaders must have a vision like the countries are developing in Africa even though with a lot of objections and interference from the colonials who are controlling Africa. But some educated presidents and leaders are unwilling to kneel in front of the colonials like the old corrupted leaders. They decided that dignity and pride were greater than money, was the power of Africa, and that they would never kneel before others even if they had to starve.

The good news is that in 2019, like in 2018, Sub-Saharan Africa will be home to several of the world's fastest-growing economies, according to the IMF. The region's growth numbers will be led again by Ethiopia, Rwanda, Ghana, Côte d'Ivoire, Senegal, Benin, Kenya, Uganda, and Burkina Faso, who remain at the top TEN.

"But still in the 21ˢᵗ century, as white supremacists as their shoe lickers, several presidents and leaders have mortgaged some African countries to the same white colonialists and ruled

that country despite famine" The country will not survive without the massacre of these leaders by the people, and these countries are an insult to Africa itself.

"The time has come for African mothers to confront these leaders with kitchen weapons crushing cassava and yam with the brooms."

How to develop Africa:

Each country can adapt to the opportunities that the Qatar Government offers to the citizen of Qatar. As part of developing and improving the infrastructure and facilities to attract foreigners, Qatar Government provided free land to the citizen of Qatar in the selected areas who can build their Towers not less than ten floors. These towers will be used for Hotels, Offices, Accommodation, etc. Within 10 to 20 years, over 200 buildings came up, starting from 20 floors to over 40 floors within the beautiful city called the Doha Corniche area (Dafna-West Bay). This long vision gives the courage to the citizen of Qatar to invest their own money in their country, and all the citizens benefit from that. You can see almost all of Qatar's well-reputed 7Star, 5Star, and 3Star Hotels. During this event, the building made Qatar more colorful.

https://www.google.com/search?rlz=1C1NHXL_enQA689 QA689&ei=t64QX7rjBKrez7sPqtauoA0&q=west+in+qatar&gs_ ssp=

Similar project:

The Pearl-Qatar: Homewww.thepearlqatar.com

The Pearl Qatar in Doha, Qatar, is an artificial island spanning nearly four square kilometers. It is the first land in Qatar to be available for freehold ownership by foreign nationals. As of 2018, there are 27,000 residents. This is one of the best tourist destinations in Qatar with excellent facilities; once you visit these places, you would like to come back again and again.

Upon these ideas becoming successful, Qatar Government started to develop the next city with the same plan. The Lusail City, Lusail is a planned city in Qatar, located on the coast, in the northern part of the municipality of Al Daayen. Lusail is located about 23 km north of the city center of Doha, just north of the West Bay Lagoon, on over 38 km², and will eventually have the infrastructure to accommodate 450,000. Many jobs were created because of these ideas, not only for the citizens but also for the foreigners. **https://www.google. com/search?gs_ssp=eJzj4tTP1TdIMk3PTTJg9OLOKS1OzM xRSM4sqQQAWfoHxQ&q=lusail+city&**

Suppose the African visionaries can adopt this option. In that case, the rich people, as well as the poor from the American diaspora, can invest, and these investors can proudly say that "I am in my own mother country of Africa."

The below-mentioned 10 Richest Billionaires can make Africa colorful and rich, and their investment will shoot up like nuclear because the opportunities are tremendous. The reason is almost all the raw materials are extracted and exploited from the African continent to another continent for centuries. **"The higher the yield, the fewer the workers in Africa."**

The Black American winners:

1. **Robert Smith** - Robert Frederick Smith is an American businessman, philanthropist, chemical engineer, and investor. He was born on December 1, 1962, in Colorado, United States.

Net worth 5 billion Dollars. He is the founder, chairman, and CEO of Vista Equity Partners.

Smith is also the founding director and President of the Fund II Foundation, which makes grants related to African American cultural preservation, human rights, environmental conservation, music education, and "sustaining the American values of entrepreneurship, empowerment, innovation, and security."

Though Smith's gift to the 2019 graduates of Morehouse College may be his most eye-catching philanthropic effort, it isn't his first. In 2017, Smith signed on to the Giving Pledge, joining a group of ultra-wealthy individuals — including Bill and Melinda Gates and Warren Buffett — who has publicly committed to giving the majority of their wealth to philanthropy. He's the first African American to sign the pledge.

2. **David Steward** - David L. Steward is an American businessman. He was born in 1951 in Chicago, Illinois, United States. Net worth 3.9 billion Dollars. He is chairman and founder of World-Wide Technology, one of the largest African-American-owned businesses in America. Steward is one of five black billionaires in America. Thelma and David Steward stand out as leaders and philanthropists in a region already noted as the most charitable in the nation. Their deep love of God and the St. Louis community has led them to support organizations that make life better and healthier for people of all ages in neighborhoods across the metro area.

3. **Oprah Winfrey** - Oprah Gail Winfrey, Net worth 2.7 billion dollars. Born January 29, 1954, Kosciusko, Mississippi, United States, is an American talk show host, actress, television producer, media executive, and philanthropist. She became one of the wealthiest and most influential women in the United States. Oprah Winfrey, formally The Oprah Winfrey Leadership Academy Foundation, is a tax-deductible charity with total assets of US$172 million. In 2006, Winfrey added US$36 million of her own money to the Foundation

4. **Michael Jordan** - Michael Jeffrey Jordan, Born February 17, 1963, in Brooklyn, New York, United States, is an American former professional basketball player and the principal owner of the Charlotte Hornets of the National Basketball Association. Michael Jordan is the world's richest athlete, with a $2.1 billion net worth. Michael Jordan is involved with various charities, including the Boys and Girls Clubs of America, UNCF/College Fund, Special Olympics, and other charitable organizations supporting children and families.

5. **Kanye West** - Kanye Omari West is an American rapper.

Network 1.3 million Dollars, Born June 8, 1977, Atlanta, Georgia, United States. Singer, songwriter, record producer, composer, and fashion designer. His music draws from various genres, including hip hop, soul, baroque pop, electro, indie rock, synth-pop, industrial, and gospel. He makes most of his money from his footwear and apparel brand, Yeezy. The streetwear brand, which sells clothing and sneakers in partnership with Adidas, was valued at $3 billion by Bank of America in 2019. West is the brand's sole owner, according to Forbes.

6. **Jay-Z -** Shawn Corey Carter, better known by his stage name Jay-Z, is an American rapper, songwriter, record executive, entrepreneur, businessman, and record producer. He was born December 4, 1969, in Brooklyn, New York, United States. **Net worth 1 billion dollars**. The Shawn Carter Foundation was formed in 2003 to improve the opportunities for at-risk youth and has since donated more than $4 million to community and scholarship programs. Throughout his years of touring, JAY-Z has often leveraged his shows to support people and causes.

7. **DIDDY-** (Sean Combs) Diddy is an American rapper, singer, songwriter, record producer, executive, entrepreneur, and actor. Combs was born November 4, 1969, in New York City but was raised in Mount Vernon, New York. **Net worth 900 million dollars**. As the Chairman and CEO of Combs Enterprises, he has a diverse portfolio of businesses and investments covering the music, fashion, fragrance, beverage, marketing, film,

television, and media industries with companies such as Bad Boy Worldwide Entertainment Group

8. **Sheela Johnson** - Sheila Crump Johnson is an American businesswoman Born January 25, 1949, in McKeesport, Pennsylvania, United States, Co-founder of BET, CEO of Salamander Hotels and Resorts, and the first African-American woman Net worth 820 million Dollars

Sheila Johnson has said, "If we're going to improve women's lives worldwide – and I believe we must – then we have to stretch beyond ourselves. We have to challenge ourselves, and we have to challenge others."

President Obama appointed Johnson to the President's Committee on the Arts and Humanities, an appropriate fit for a woman who has dedicated her career to the arts, education, and human rights. She also sits on the boards of Americans for the Arts, the Jackie Robinson Foundation, and the University Of Virginia Curry School Of Education, among other prominent charitable organizations.

9. **Dr. Dre** is an American rapper, record producer, audio engineer, record executive, entrepreneur, and actor. Born February 18, 1965, Compton, California, United States Net worth 820 million Dollars. He is the founder and CEO of Aftermath Entertainment and Beats Electronics. Dr. Dre began his career as a DJ in clubs around Compton and South-Central Los Angeles. He co-founded N.W.A., which illustrated life in South Central with the album Straight Outta Compton. In 1992

10. **Eldrick Tont - Tiger Woods** is an American professional golfer.

Total Net worth is estimated ed over 800 million Dollars.

Born December 30, 1975, in Cypress, California, United States, He is tied for first in PGA Tour wins, ranks second in men's major championships, and holds numerous golf records. Tiger is regarded as one of the greatest golfers in the history of Sports. Woods is widely regarded as one of the greatest golfers and one of the most famous athletes. Woods owns a restaurant and sports lounge in his hometown called The Woods Jupiter that he opened in 2015 and has continued to expand his course design business launched over a decade ago, emphasizing playability and fun.

TGR Foundation was established in 1996 by Tiger Woods and his father, Earl Woods, to create and support community-based programs that improve the health, education, and welfare of all children in America. ... The Tiger Woods Foundation is about empowering minorities, especially underprivileged minority students.

All the African leaders need to send the invitation to this business tycoon or meet them personalities to invest in Africa rather than begging and taking huge loans from China or other countries. Let them put their investments to Africa and must give the contract to the African diaspora without even tendering, which will benefit both the diaspora and the African country.

- Let Robert Smith's Charity donate to black African Children who are really in need of academic help. Robert Smith can be a savior to the African continent by bringing up the children of Africa from 54 Countries.
- Let David Steward's Telecom Technology and computer support serve the entire 55 African countries.
- Let Oprah Winfrey spend little time producing a film about Africa and its people to show how the black people can do and Winfrey Leadership Academy Foundation to serve the entire 54 Countries in Africa.
- Let Michael Jordan's charitable fund be used for the African children to build a basketball club to develop African children throughout 54 countries in Africa.

If you give a fish to a poor man, he will eat and wait for the next fish from you for the next meal. If you teach him how to fish, that poor man will feel for himself and his entire family; sometimes, he may think about feeding his neighbors.

These Rich people's one-year Charity donations are sufficient to build Africa rich. The gifts can be your investment because when you invest these donations into business, many educated African children will get job opportunities. So that he and his family will enjoy the benefit, we cannot change all at once; let it be one by one.

"You will rejoice in how much you have donated rather than how much you have earned."

Today or tomorrow, we must leave this earth by the time we will never take our personal belongings or assets with us other than the soul. Only the accounts of our good and evil deeds can be found in our heaven or hell accounts. But the good deeds we have done for this world while we are alive will remain on this earth even if we die; our name will not survive because we put some billions in the bank account and died.

BIBLE: LUKE 16-21 "The ground of a certain rich man yielded an abundant harvest. [17] He thought to himself, 'What shall I do? I have no place to store my crops.'

[18] "Then he said, 'This is what I'll do. I will tear down my barns, build bigger ones, and store my surplus grain there. [19] And I'll tell myself, "You have plenty of grain laid up for many years. Take life easy; eat, drink and be merry."'

[20] "But God said to him, 'You fool! This very night your life will be demanded from you. Then who will get what you have prepared for yourself?'

[21] "This is how it will be with whoever stores up things for themselves but is not rich toward God."

"Remember today you are overshadowed by the heat experienced by your ancestor."

All the Rich Black American diaspora and the diaspora around Europe and other parts of the world must realize that your DNA is in Africa, not America, Europe, or any other parts of the world. You must recap the film of African history at least 400 years ago. Then you will know how your forefathers reached America and other parts of the world. You and your early generation may be born in the place where you are living.

(The House apologizes to African-Americans on behalf of the people of the United States…for the fundamental injustice, cruelty, brutality, and inhumanity of slavery…and for the wrongs committed against them and their ancestors; By Jim Crow.)

HUMAN SLAVERY

Imagine if this was you and your father and mother. Would you be happy? By knowing all this history, as an African, how can you sit comfortably enjoying your wealth by forgetting the past African forefathers? It was you before five centuries, your DNA and same soul; you are just a copy of it. Unfortunately, some African men would love sleeping too much when they get enough comfort and don't bother about the past of their ancestors. This attitude has to be changed to build Africa.

"Let me describe one thing I encountered in Africa."

The body of an older man was found in pieces on the side of the road during my visit to an African country while traveling from one state to another by car. I do not want to reveal the name of that country.

I have asked my driver why this body is here on the road?

The man said it is common for few of the elders to have no one to look after them, Someone may have been hit on the road, and due to the high cost of funeral expenses, he had been left in the street, and then the municipal authorities will come and pick them up. It was a real shock for me at that time.

"Could this man be the father of children who have forgotten their parents and are now as a diaspora in the USA or Europe or elsewhere?"

Similarly, some parents may be waiting for the arrival of their abandoned children?

Many of us who are reluctant to give a kiss while alive have seen our parents or siblings kissing their bodies when they are dead. Why our kisses to them after death? If it is given while they are alive, their hearts will rejoice, and tears of joy will flow from them. So many parents in the world today want a kiss of love from their children. How many kisses did our parents give us when we were babies, and how many kisses did we give them? Instead of offering flowers and candles in their graves when they are dead, are there any parents who would not be happy if given light and a bouquet while alive?

Some studies show that 4-year-olds ask as many as 200 to 300 questions daily. Warren Berger, the author of A More Beautiful Question, says kids ask an average of 40,000 questions between the ages of 2 and 5. But when we become adults, and our parents become old, even if they asktwo2 questions twice, we get angry.... Was there like this?

"Understand the truth that there is no greater treasure in life than the blessing of parents."

WHAT YOU SEE IN YOURSELF IS WHAT YOU SEE IN THE WORLD"

B<small>RANDING A</small> N<small>EGRESS AT THE</small> R<small>IO</small> P<small>ONGO</small>
From a wood engraving in Canot's *Twenty Years of an African Slaver,*
New York, 1854

What more can you expect from the colonialists?

The New York Times Magazine

Four hundred years after being enslaved, Africans were first brought to Virginia; Most Americans don't know the entire history of slavery. **https://www.nytimes.com/interactive/2019/08/19/magazine/history-slavery-smithsonian.html**
Curated by Mary Elliott
All text by Mary Elliott and Jazmine Hughes -Aug. 19, 2019

The present African generation is the luckiest even though with a few sacrifices you have gone through in this century. Because many of your forefathers and mothers who were enslaved by the white colonialists that day died on the way without food or water and were s shackled with chains. The Fathers witnessed their wife and daughters being raped in front of them. Those who opposed were brutally tortured and thrown into the middle of the sea. It had been said that if the ship had not reached the appointed schedule, the colonialists would use the human enslaved person's flesh for food. It has also been reported that some infectious diseases attack any enslaved people who are killed or thrown alive into the Mediterranean Sea without a conscience.

After surviving all these hardships and suffering, they came to the United States and similar countries and lived as enslaved people for centuries. All Northern states had abolished slavery by 1805; sometimes, abolition was gradual, and hundreds of people were still enslaved in the Northern states as late as the 1840 Census. The 13th Amendment, adopted on December 18, 1865, officially abolished slavery, but freed Black peoples' status in the post-war South remained precarious, and significant challenges awaited during the Reconstruction period.

At last, Martin Luther King, Jr. was the leader of the **civil rights movement** and led nonviolent protests in the 1950s and 60s, fighting for equality for African **Americans**. Thus, Martin Luther King sacrificed himself for the world's black people. Who will be the next Martin Luther King? Who was the next Nelson Mandela to protect the right of African descendants?

- Does this mean that not all Black Americans were enslaved three or four generations ago?
- Doesn't the distinction between black and white exist in America in this 21st century?
- You don't need to see the video of George Floyd, a police officer's knee on his neck for 9 minutes as he struggled for his dying breaths, to know that black people are three times more likely to be killed by police than are white people.
- Racism and casteism are mental illnesses often used when the upper castes are convinced that they will lose power. Racist people's percentage may be less than 10%, but the rest of the good white people are also sometimes victims because of white supremacy; they are also probably the victims of black hatred.

It is not the time to take revenge but to think wise and build your kingdom, Africa. Even if your enslaved forefathers and mothers were brutally killed by the white colonialist in America or other countries, their souls would never wish to stay in America or other countries; their souls never wish to go out of Africa because colonialists can kill only the body, not the soul. Did they not suffer like that? The souls of your forefathers and mothers living in Africa are calling you along with your children's wish to return home.

Africa is your home. You better build a house and settle in Africa. No more white colonialists will come and attack again. Because your forefathers and mothers were so generous in those days, they never knew that these colonialists came like priests with smiling faces with white bodies and hearts to colonize and capture them as enslaved people. They thought all human beings were as good as Africans and did not care what lies, deceit, or deception were. But your generation now is intelligent and capable of finding out the wrong people and how to resist yourself. But most people living in Africa are still generous and fear fighting the existing colonialists looting the assets from Africa until now. As African diaspora, how much do you love them?

Those big ships from Africa to America took over 40 days; all these 40 days, these forefathers came here by boat, rowing on their hands without food or water, and were subjected to severe persecution when asked for food or water. Otherwise, all those who opposed it must have been massacred. Less than 30 or 40% of the enslaved people survived until the end of the journey to America.

"The Mediterranean Sea must have caused the death of millions of Africans."

The brothers of many of these captives may not know you today but with your blood and your DNA still living in some part of Africa. It is your responsibility to find them. You are so generous; therefore, you are donging many charities in America or elsewhere. **"Charity must begin from Home."** A portion of your charity can be spent on your brothers and sisters who are still struggling for food in Africa.

For many centuries the European claimed that they were feeding Africa, but in effect, they were looting one ton of Gold or equal asset and bringing one ton of rice or pasta to Africa.

They are giving the food not because they like African people; this is only to protect their looting assets. The more money they are spending not to support African people but the terrorist to make noise and kill them to make the people not look in the mining area. Media, those supporting them, and some religious leaders sometimes use religion as a weapon if the local people try to resist.

If you travel to Africa, you can see some mothers and sisters carrying their babies on their backs and carrying over 30 to 40 kilos of luggage on their heads to sell the items in the street to feed their families. You can also see young girls who are supposed to go to school, but it's miserable due to poverty; they are in the street selling few things for their daily living. It may be not from your family or DNA if suppose some of them are from your DNA, is that good for you????????

"When you spend the charity to the rich country, it is like a side dish on the full course buffet lunch or dinner, but when you do the same amount of charity to the poor country, that side dish is going to be their rich main course meal."

May your DNA belong to some of these countries?

North Africa:
Algeria
Egypt
Libya
Mauritania
Morocco
Sahrawi Arab Democratic Republic (Western Sahara)
Tunisia

Southern Africa
Angola
Botswana
Eswatini (Swaziland)
Lesotho
Malawi
Mozambique
Namibia
South Africa
Zambia
Zimbabwe

East Africa
Comoros
Djibouti
Eritrea
Ethiopia
Kenya
Madagascar
Mauritius
Rwanda
Seychelles
Somalia
South Sudan
Sudan

Tanzania
Uganda

West Africa
Benin
Burkina Faso
Cabo Verde
Côte d'Ivoire
The Gambia
Ghana
Guinea-Bissau
Guinea
Liberia
Mali
Niger
Nigeria
Senegal
Sierra Leone
Togo

Central Africa
Burundi
Cameroon
The Central African Republic
Chad
Congo Republic

WHO MADE AFRICA POOR?

The slave trade existed even before 2000 years ago until AD1600 in a small way; it went to Arab countries and Asian countries. But with the advent of the Europeans, the slave trade began on a large scale. In 1619 the first enslaved African arrived in Virginia, the USA, brought by the British with enslaved peoples captured from the Portuguese. These enslaved people were usually baptized in Africa before embarking.

Although the slave trade took place in Africa, Africa was more prosperous than any other continent. Egypt, Sudan, Mali, Ethiopia, Kenya, Tanzania, Rhodesia (Zimbabwe), Mauritius, Liberia, Nigeria, Morocco, Tunisia, Libya, Algeria, etc. The wealth of Mali and Empire Mansa Musa's gold-plated luxuries pilgrim trip to Macca has opened the eyes of Europeans to Africa beginning with French occupation, and until today it continues. From then on, Africa began to decline and become poorer. To know more about Mali and slavery, please refers to **"THE HIDDEN VOICE OF AFRICA"** Author: Sebastian Joseph – Published by Outskirts Press – USA and Partridge Publishing India.

In ancient times, gold or silver was not synonymous with wealth. Gold, silver, copper, and iron were used only to make coins, palaces, thrones, tombs, or military weapons. At that time, the wealthiest countries were the ones that could produce food and clothes. The Climatically blessed North African region, with the presence of the Nile River, was the biggest producer and exporter of crops, such as wheat, barley, animal and grapes, cotton, etc. It is linked to the Middle East and the Fertile Crescent, and the agricultural techniques of that region were adopted wholesale. Later this agricultural business spread to all other African areas.

"Sometimes man loses control over himself during the journey of life. Then everything is judged and becomes inactive. This is the biggest myth in the world."

From the 15th Century onward, the European started colonizing Africa. Before that, the Portuguese first began to kidnap people from the west coast of Africa and take those they enslaved back to Europe. Since then, the Europeans have extended their aggression to all African countries other than Liberia and Ethiopia.

From 1884, the Europeans started extracting all kinds of Minerals, including uranium, from Africa. During this period, the Europeans used all the Africans as their slaves in the mining areas and their needs. They did not consider the African human race list; they treated the Africans worse than animals. They killed or brutally punished millions of people who disobeyed their command. The wealth that killed and usurped the people of Africa paved the way for the destruction of Europe's ideas. Africa's curse was World War I and World War II. World War I &II was the most destructive war in history. Estimates of those killed vary from 35 million to 60 million. The total for Europe alone was 15 million to 20 million. The total death worldwide is 2-3 Billion only because of this nasty colonialist.

It is known that the Belgium Empire Leopold II of Belgium invasion killed 75% of the Congolese. Germany committed genocide in Africa 40 years before the Holocaust of the European Jews. In 1904 and 1905, the Ova Herero and Nama people of central and southern Namibia rose against colonial rule and dispossession in what was then called German Southwest Africa. The revolt was brutally crushed. By 1908, 80% of the Ova Herero and 50% of the Nama had died of starvation, thirst, overwork, and exposure to harsh climates.

Survivors of Namibia's Herero tribe surrendered after a battle with German forces.

In the recent update on May 2021, Germany had offered Namibia $1.3 billion as compensation for their brutality to the Namibian people. At least Germany found their mistake, but all other colonizers are still trying to loot from these countries shamelessly and talking about human rights.

Berlin West Africa Conference, a series of negotiations (Nov. 15, 1884–Feb. 26, 1885) at Berlin, in which the major European nations met to decide all questions connected with the Congo River basin in Central Africa.

In 1884, the Berlin Conference was convened to discuss African colonization and to set up international guidelines for making claims to African land to avoid conflict between European powers. But to Africa, it was just a play to trap Africans. Under the Berlin Treaty made by these invading whites, they brought Africa under their jurisdiction at the whim of everyone. The Congo Conference or West Africa Conference regulated European colonization and trade in Africa during the New Imperialism period and coincided with Germany's sudden emergence as an imperial power. At this meeting, the colonized divided the 54

Countries of the African continent and implemented their regular game of divide and rule policy.

"For every action, there is an equal and opposite reaction."

This is the universal truth of the earth, Man-made castes, religions, and human atrocities have no place here.

After World War II, the starving Europeans resumed their hegemony without leaving Africa. In 1957 with the leader of the struggle led by Kwame Nkrumah, Ghana became the first independent country in Africa. They were followed by other countries in Africa, becoming independent.

But before the Europeans gave freedom to the Africans, they implemented their divide and rule policies all over Africa. Before they returned to their homeland, by force, they imposed their laws, the worst of which is still France. Belgium and France, then and now, continue their atrocities against the African people in this 21st century. Killed or ousted all the leaders who have tried to develop Africa in these short periods of sixty years. Under this guide, African political leaders are using the United Nations Peacekeeping Force for their protection.

- Is it possible to believe that it is true that even the United States does not know the fact that Africa does not control airspace in the region?
- The colonialist's Chartered flights are coming inside the forest ground and taking all the looted minerals from the Republic of Congo and the Central African Republic every day without the United Nations' knowledge?
- Every child in Africa knows this looting has been going on for years and years.

In most African countries, especially in this 21st century, the Central African Republic and the Congo, billion dollars worth of gold, copper, cobalt, uranium, diamonds, etc., are still being smuggled in. Is it true that other countries do not see this mineral trafficking or because they are deliberately silent in fear of these countries?

It is said that all human beings and animals need to fill their stomachs. Still, in the meanwhile, the python does not know the quantity and its capacity to serve its stomachs, swallows the prey completely, and lies motionless there until the food is digested. Fortunately, if no one sees the food until it is digested, the python will escape, or someone will kill them. The same thing that happened to python will indeed happen to the colonialists who are still trying to seize the food that the Africans are entitled to; it may be at the hands of the Africans because those poor old Africans are not going to face you now.

Now you will be confronted by a group of young African children and the African diaspora who can understand the lies learned in the United States and many parts of Europe. That will be an African's power, equivalent to ten ordinary people's power.

For ages, European colonialists have plundered property in Africa and branded Africans as poor. You have enriched your country with the wealth of Africa. In return, you have given Africa several rogue leaders and laws that benefit only the Europeans and weapons that can destroy the whole of Africa. It is still dangerous for you to interfere in the internal affairs of Africa; this is just a hint. **He who has ears, let him hear.**

Whites still dominate South Africa, with real Africans living on their sidewalks and in unsafe homes. But white immigrants in South Africa own mansions, acres of farms, and gold mines. The law, enacted before whites granted independence to Africa, is still in force.

Julius Sello Malema is a South African politician who is a Member of Parliament and the President and Commander-in-Chief of the Economic Freedom Fighters, a South African political party he founded in July 2013. He served as President of the African National Congress Youth League from 2008 to 2012. Africa needs leaders like these, at least 100 Malema's fighting for equal justice for African black people.

Whites still occupy hectares of farms in Zimbabwe; In the 1880s, the British arrived with Cecil Rhodes' British South Africa Company. In 1898, the name Southern Rhodesia was adopted. In 1888, British colonialist Cecil Rhodes obtained a concession for mining rights from King Lobengula of the Ndebele peoples. These are all properties that the British Cork preferred, killing and expelling its natives. Many have been used for centuries to sell enslaved people to foreign countries or to enslave them into their formulas.

These colonialists, who told women who had given birth without conscience to run away with the new bone babies, are now talking nonsense about human rights. What right do they have to talk about human rights? If one black speaks out against whites, many channels will come to ask about human rights. The truth is that when millions of blacks were massacred, no humanitarians thought, and still, no one was there to ask the whites about human rights. They know that without Africa, these whites will starve (I am not against the good white people, I am talking only about the thief who is plundering Africa), and they still live by killing and plundering blacks for their survival. The same tactic is used in Africa, the Middle East, the Far East, and worldwide.

At the time of independence to Zimbabwe in 1980, more than 40% of the country's farmed land comprised approximately 5,000 white farms. Agriculture provided 40% of the country's GDP and 60% of its foreign earnings. Major export products included tobacco, beef, sugar, cotton, and maize. Land reform in Zimbabwe officially began in 1980 with the signing of the Lancaster House Agreement to more equitably distribute land between black subsistence farmers and white Zimbabweans of European ancestry. They had traditionally enjoyed superior political and economic status.

When white colonialists occupied the land from Zimbabwean farmers, nobody compensated black farmers. But per the Lancaster House Agreement Zimbabwean government took back the land from white farmers. They claim billions of dollars as compensation, and the international union supports white farmers.

- What kind of justice is this??
- Did white people bring any land to Zimbabwe from Europe?
- For the whites one justice and for the blacks another justice??

In many countries, United Nations are imposing sanctions.

The Security Council can take action to maintain or restore international peace and security under Chapter VII of the United Nations Charter. Sanctions measures, under Article 41, encompass a broad range of enforcement options that do not involve using armed force. Since 1966, the Security Council has established 30 sanctions regimes in Southern Rhodesia, South Africa, the former Yugoslavia, Haiti, Iraq, Angola, Rwanda, Sierra Leone, Somalia and Eritrea, Eritrea and Ethiopia, Liberia, D.R.Congo, Côte d'Ivoire, Sudan, Lebanon, DPRK, Iran, Libya, Guinea-Bissau, Yemen, South Sudan, and Mali.

My question to United Nations is why the ordinary people in that country should struggle because of some leaders' mistakes. All these country groups are using the latest weapons.

- Who is supplying all these weapons?
- Who is the manufacturer?
- Who is struggling?
- If sanctions protect that country and the world, why are you allowing the weapons to come there? And that weapons are in the hands of the children even.
- Sanction means weapon selling?
- How many people's life, house, infrastructure, hospitals, and so on and on were destroyed?
- How many countries are peaceful because of restoring international peace and security under Chapter VII of the United Nations?

Soon after imposing sanctions, two groups of weapon suppliers within the United Nations VETO power members will take place that positioning to bombard and destroy that country.

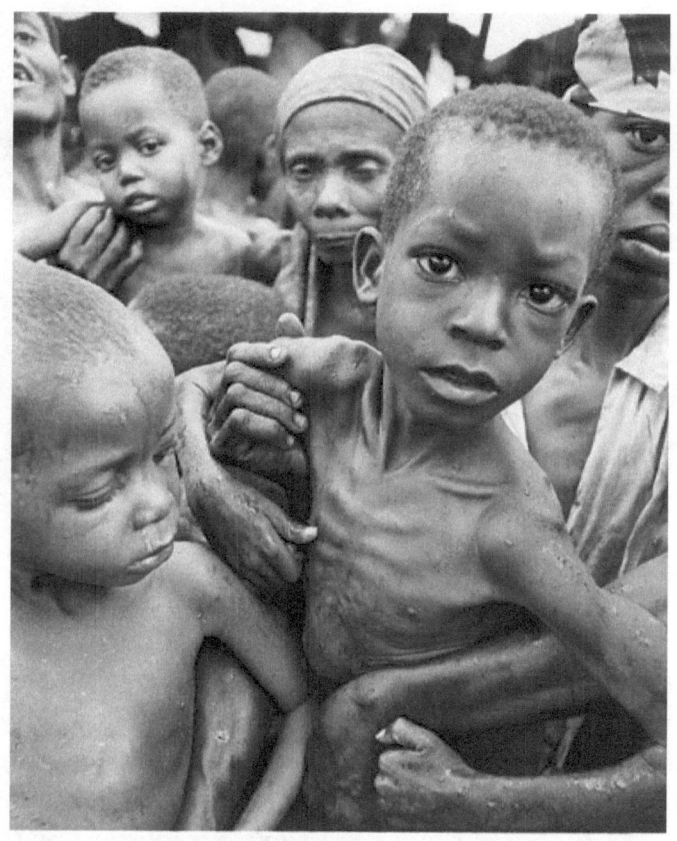

Colonialists, still not enough to drink their blood?

WHERE IS GOD? WHERE ARE THE RELIGIOUS LEADERS WHO PREACH ABOUT GOD AND RELIGION TO REACH HEAVEN? TO REACH HEAVEN, YOU GOT TO DIE FIRST. LET THE TERRORIST LEADERS DIE FIRST AND GO TO HEAVEN BETTER.

WHERE ARE THE UNICEF/UNITED NATIONS LEADERS WHO COLLECT BILLIONS OF DOLLARS EVERY YEAR? THE MONEY COLLECTED IS USED FOR A FEW THEIFS ENJOYING.

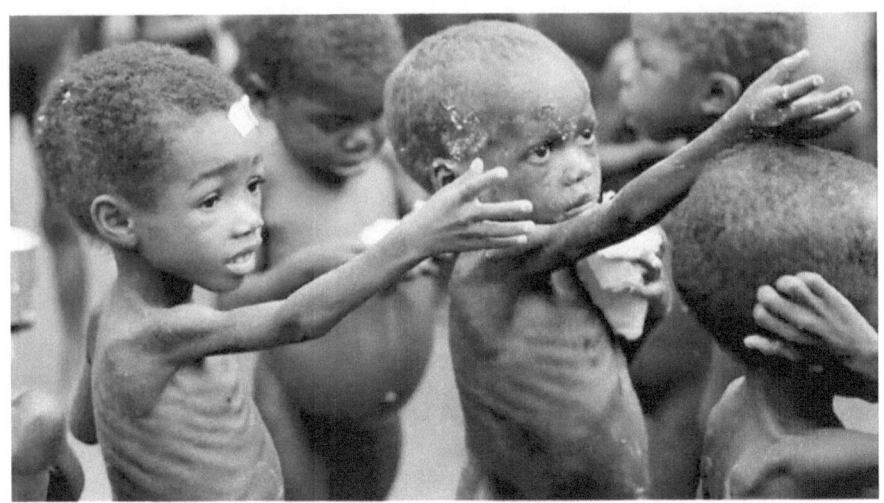

THE REAL OWNERS OF AFRICAN WEALTH ARE STILL BEGGING

What mistake did these African people make to the world? How long, who is responsible???

The real owners of Africa's wealth are still struggling.

"Shameful colonialists and some black leaders who want to drink the blood of these men too" No religion or God can forgive you...................

Those who have eyes see, and those who have ears hear; if you have a little conscience, let these poor people live as human beings. They are not coming to plunder your property; let them live peacefully in their own country.

All these countries' children are dying every minute, all mother's breasts are dried with no milk of the infant's lack of food, no houses or buildings left.

- Let us know if one country improves because of your imposed sanctions rule?
- Is this so-called peacekeeping?
- Then, what is the meaning of these sanctions?

If some white colonialists decided to spoil one country, they convinced the United Nations with their power to break that country to impose their revenge against that country or the leaders.

- What mistakes did the people of the country make?

This is no more acceptable if the United Nations intends to keep peace in the world.

This is as equal as some countries decided to lock down to prevent COVID19 without securing food and necessary things. Then again, people sat in fear as if dying of starvation. The world's nations must react against this law. Otherwise, only the agenda of the colonialists will survive in this world.

"It is their policy of the white colonialists to make the war each other to sell the weapons they need and the medicine they need when the nations are at war, even the coffin for them when they die."
Many of the leaders who still do not understand their tactics rule Africa. It is a shame for the African continent still some of the shameful leaders of Africa licked the shoes of whites for little bribes and surrendered the countries under their legs.

Who is Poor?????

If these countries are poor, then why did the Europeans Colonize Africa?????

As a first step, African leaders must rename African names by removing all the Phones (francophone, Anglophone, Lusophone, this phone, that phone, etc.) ...Africa no longer requires these phones.... Africa needs only Afro phones. Also, Africa must bring back their old name for their states if it is not African.

India had done this already by bringing it back to its name. For example, Bombay- Mumbai, Madras-Chennai, Bangalore-Bengaluru, etc. Who are the African leaders afraid of now that the whole world is with them?

France is rich because of the African Colonialism of these Countries; they called it Francophone countries. Benin, Burkina Faso, Burundi, Cameroon, Chad, the Ivory Coast, the Democratic Republic of the Congo, Djibouti, Equatorial Guinea, Madagascar, Mali, Monaco, Niger, Rwanda, Senegal, Togo. French is their first language even though they have their local languages.

No more French Frank in France since long years, they use Euro Currency. But most of these countries are using French Frank. All the currencies are printed from France; these African countries have no authorization to print their cash within the country or from anywhere else.

- Is it because Africa was poor? The German conquered for decades the six principal colonies of German Africa, along with native kingdoms and policies, which were the legal precedents for the modern states of Burundi, Cameroon, Namibia, Rwanda, Tanzania, and Togo?

These are the assets looted from Africa to Germany Tin, Phosphates, Iron Ore, Diamonds, Gemstones, Gold, Nickel, Natural gas, Coal,

This is the time to save Africa from the present colonialists; if not, it will never be possible. All the African Diaspora around the world must unite and take action to take back their own country from the colonialist who pulled their forefathers with chains and brought them as slaves to the place where they are staying now. Africa is your country; the mother of Africa is calling you back; pack up to start the journey now.

One thing you should not forget when you go to Africa is your unity; this is not the time to look at race, religion, caste, color, or size (**Some people within the black African DNA are more racist than the white racist, they talk about racism in a good way in front of the people but their hearts are black) because** this is the weapon that the colonialists ever used as their weapon, sprinkle yourself in the name of caste, color, and ethnicity. A great example of this is the recent massacres in many African countries.

"Yet you are not one for your Gods, and if your Gods are powerful, you do not need to save God. God knows how to save himself."

Remember, Religion is the biggest dangerous weapon ever used in human history for political benefit.

"THE MOST BEAUTIFUL FIG MAY CONTAIN A WORM"

Africa has never been poor and will never be poor. The ugly colonialists who invaded Africa made the people of Africa poor.

Zambia or Chambia? Some Zambian citizens and Africans are asking this question about Zambia. The total population of Zambia is more than 18 million. One million Chinese people are in Zambia, controlling the significant cities and businesses in Zambia. You may see several Chinese shops and businesses than Zambian Citizens. And in the town, the number of Chinese people's movement, you may think you are in China, not Africa. African diaspora must understand that if Zambia is poor, why are all these Chinese there? Well, some of the other countries in the Middle East have different nationalities than their citizens that countries with only one or more natural resources, which are Oil and Gas like Saudi Arabia, Qatar, Kuwait, United Arab Emirates, Bahrain, Oman, etc. but those countries are making sure that their citizens are in the government jobs and well-protected life living, the rest of the opportunities are offered to other nationalities to work for them to protect and generate the income for that governments.

But in African countries, cases are just the opposite, and other nationalities are coming to do business, occupying comfortable positions, and offering complex labor jobs to the local citizens. In effect, again, the African people are until now living as enslaved people working for somebody even though they are the owner of tremendous natural resources in their own country, which nobody can deny. Who is responsible?

The wealthy African diaspora must find the answer to this.

CHAPTER ~ 6

RELIGION AND COLONIAL EXPLORATION

Knowing some of the history and truth of the African Diaspora about Africa is essential. History has shown that religious propaganda and conversion have not brought many benefits to the poor in Africa.

Religion in pre-Islamic Arabia included indigenous animistic-polytheistic beliefs, Christianity, Judaism, Mandaeism, and Iranian faiths of Zoroastrianism, Mithraism, and Manichaeism. Following the conquest of North Africa by Muslim Arabs in the 7th century, Islam spread throughout West Africa via merchants, traders, scholars, and missionaries. African rulers either tolerated the religion or converted to it themselves.

The word Hindu is an exonym, and while Hinduism has been called the oldest religion in the world, many practitioners refer to their religion as Sanātana Dharma, "the eternal way," which refers to the idea that its origins lie beyond human history, as revealed in the Hindu texts.

"God must dwell in the minds and hearts of every human being."

God's belief existed even before Jewish, Christianity, and Muslim religions, History proves "Year BC-(Before Christ, 2000 years ago)" people believed in Hindu or Greek Gods. Greek pantheon consists of 12 deities who were said to reside at Mount Olympus: Zeus, Hera, Aphrodite, Apollo, Ares, Artemis, Athena, Demeter, Dionysus, Hephaestus, Hermes, and Poseidon.

Indigenous African beliefs before Jewish, Christian, and Muslim religions:

- Nana-Buluku. Nana-Buluku is a creator god. ...
- Obatala. Obatala is the son of the sky god, Olorun, who tasked Obatala with creating the world. ...
- Olorun. Olorun, in many regards, is the Zeus or Jehovah of the Yoruba pantheon. ...
- Yemaya. is the goddess of childbirth and water. ...
- Oba., Oko. Osanyin. Olokun etc.

It is safe to say that pre-religious times were, in fact, the good old days in Africa. This is because there was no system of enslaving human beings in these times. People captured in battle were enslaved and subject to the law of the day. Later religions described slavery as trade, legal, and God permitted it. If this is God's decision, then most of the victims of slavery are of African descent.

- **Does this mean that God had any prejudice against the African people?**
- **Did God hate these new gods or the African people?**
- **So why are these religions and these gods of African descent, and aren't those old gods enough for Africans?**
- **Does this mean that religions are not meant to protect the interests of specific communities or individuals?**

"No one can deny that in the name of God, all religions have plundered and tied with chains enslaved people of African descent exported to many lands.

"In effect, none of the religions helped the poor people of Africa until now."

It is one of the fundamental rights of every person to believe in any god or religion. God is a concept and belief, and no human has ever seen God in person. Even claiming to have seen it in person is the belief of the person who saw it or on the dream of his faith. The first thing propagandists need to do is change the hunger of the people who have joined before inviting new people to join the religion.

Missionaries saw the voyages to Africa by their governments as an opportunity for them to spread the teaching of the Christian faith. They used some of the British Empire's resources, and then, in turn, the empire coerced them to use their education to subdue the Africans. European missionaries wanted to spread Christianity and teach it to less educated and wealthy people in Africa as one cause for imperialism - They mainly saw it as their duty to be carried out, and it is commonly referred to as "The White Man's Burden" They paved the way for explorers to claim African colonies for European countries.

Colonialism is the policy of a country seeking to extend or retain its authority over other people or territories, generally with the aim of economic dominance. In the process of colonization, colonizers may impose their religion, economics, and other cultural practices on indigenous peoples. Christianity and colonialism are often intertwined as they share the state religions of the colonial powers, and in many ways, they acted as the religious weapons of those forces. In some areas, almost all of the colony's population were removed from their traditional belief systems and turned into the Christian faith, which the colonizers used as a reason to destroy other religions, enslave the natives, and exploit the lands and seas. In many ways, they acted as the "religious arms" of those powers.

As Europeans moved beyond exploration and into colonization of the Americas, they brought changes to virtually every aspect of the land and its people, from trade and hunting to warfare and personal property. European goods, ideas, and diseases shaped the changing continent. During imperial expansion, religious people sometimes set out to convert new members of their religion and, thus, their empire. Christian missionaries from Europe, for example, established churches in conquered territories during the nineteenth century. In doing so, they also spread Western cultural values.

It is essential to write the actual African history book within Africa with a team of African people to teach to the upcoming generation of

Africa because the present history book may be found written by either Europeans or some other continental people.

The African continent has been the wealthiest continent ever since ancient times (by the way, until today, Africa is the wealthiest continent in the world. Still, no information about Africa was available to other continents. Europeans always believe that they are superior to any other nation. In the beginning, the Roman Emperor held this supremacy kingdom and colonized the whole of Europe. Later all other countries in Europe united and implemented the same formula to occupy other countries, including America, Asia, and Africa, with their white supremacy and colonization.

Before 2000, Africa had long been synonymous with wealth; rich means those who can produce food crops, fruits, oil, salt, animal meat, etc., and the old Africans had enough food to eat. During this period, no other country except Asia was known to be rich. During those days, Gold, silver, copper, or other metals were used to build coins, weapons, or a palace. Even then, gold deposits were highest in Africa. Africa was under poverty during the period of the slave trade and the Arab and European colonization. From that period until now, this brutality continued in Africa from the European colonialists.

Today, gold is highly reserved by the colonialists of Italy = 2,451.8 tonnes and

France = 2,436.0 tonnes which do not have a single grain of gold in their homeland. **Thanks to Africa for making Europe rich with African gold and natural resources.**

Countries and kings in Africa were more prosperous than the present billionaires today.

These are few wealthiest people in Africa before colonialism,

Sundiata Keita, 1190-1255 born in Niani, **Guinea,** was a powerful prince and founder of the Mali Empire known as Sundiata the Hero, The Lion King.

Sunni Ali, also known as Sunni Ali Ber, was born in Ali Kolon. He reigned from about 1464 to 1492. Sunni Ali was the first king of the Songhai Empire. West Africa 15th–16th century, centered on the middle reaches of the Niger River in what is now central Mali and eventually extended west to the Atlantic coast and east into Niger and Nigeria.

Mansa Musa, 1312-1337, was the tenth Mansa of the Mali Empire, an Islamic West African state. The net worth of approximately US$418 billion. He has been described as the wealthiest individual of the Middle Ages. At the time of Musa's ascension to the throne, Mali primarily consisted of the territory of the former Ghana Empire, which Mali had conquered. The famous Malian ruler Mansa Musa made a pilgrimage to Mecca.

Ibn Battuta, 1304-1369 was a Muslim Berber Moroccan scholar and explorer who traveled the medieval world widely. Over thirty years, Ibn Battuta visited most of the Islamic world and many non-Muslim lands, including Central Asia, Southeast Asia, India, and China.

Abu Bakr II (fl. 14th century), also spelled Abubakri and known as Mansa Qu, may have been the ninth Mansa of the Mali Empire.

Askia Muhammad Toure, 1493–1528 born in Futa Tooro **Senegal,** also known as Askia the Great, was an emperor, military commander, and political reformer of the Songhai Empire in the late 15th century. He was from the Soninke ethnic group.

Muammar Mohammed Abu Minyar al-Gaddafi, 1961-2011 was a Libyan revolutionary, politician, and political theorist. Net worth: US$200 billion in 2011, estimated.

During 14th to 16th centuries, most of the European countries were poor also, with deadly pandemics like the plague and Spanish Flue killing millions of people. They are afraid that all the Europeans will be wiped out.

Following are the death cause of deceases in Europe,

The Black Death was a devastating global epidemic of bubonic plague that struck Europe and Asia in the mid-1300s. The plague arrived in Europe in October 1347, when 12 ships from the Black Sea docked at the Sicilian port of Messina. One of the worst plagues in history arrived at Europe's shores in 1347. Five years later, some 25 to 50 million people were dead. Nearly 700 years after the Black Death swept through Europe, it still haunts the world as the worst-case scenario for an epidemic. The plague arrived in Western Europe in 1347 and in England in 1348. It faded away in the early 1350s. It ended in 1353.

While it's unlikely that the "Spanish Flu" originated in Spain, scientists are still unsure of its source. France, China, and Britain have all been suggested as the potential birthplace of the virus, as has the United States, where the first known case was reported at a military base in Kansas on March 11, 1918.

The 1918 influenza pandemic caused an estimated 50 million to 100 million deaths worldwide. The virus that caused the 1918 pandemic probably sprang from North American domestic and wild birds, not from mixing humans and swine. While the global pandemic lasted for two years, a significant number of deaths were packed into three fierce months in the fall of 1918. The Kings and Queens paid and equipped missionaries. They financed them to go to America, Africa, and Asia, which were less populated during those days and had more natural resources. They were subdued and ordered to bring their natural resources to Europe.

These are some of the explorers who made the financial foundation for Europe.

- Christopher Columbus
- Vasco de Gama
- Nicolo deponde
- Ferdinand Magellan
- Amerigo Vespucci
- Richard Francis Bolten
- David Livingston
- Henry Stanly
- Henrik Bath
- Fredric O resell
- Mongo Park

Bartolomeo Dias, a nobleman of the Portuguese royal household, was a Portuguese explorer. He sailed around the southernmost tip of Africa in 1488, the first European to do so, setting up the route from Europe to Asia. 15th century, Bartholomew Dias' voyage to the

Cape of Good Hope in the late 15th century marked the apex of an extraordinary Portuguese expansion overseas and the start of a fateful European impact on South Africa.

Portuguese explorer Vasco de Gama becomes the first European to reach India via the Atlantic Ocean when he arrives at Calicut on the Malabar Coast. Da Gama sailed from Lisbon, Portugal, in July 1497, rounded the Cape of Good Hope, and anchored at Malindi. Malindi District was a former administrative district in the Coast Province of Kenya. Its capital was the coastal town of Malindi when it was eliminated and merged into Kilifi County in 2010 on the east coast of Africa.

The French presence in Africa dates to the 17th century. Still, the main period of colonial expansion came in the 19th century with the invasion of Ottoman Algiers in 1830, conquests in West and Equatorial Africa during the so-called scramble for Africa, and establishment protectorates in Tunisia and Morocco in the decades before the First World War. To these were added parts of German Togo and Cameroon, assigned to France as League of Nations mandates after the war. French colonial Africa encompassed the vast confederations of French West Africa 1895 and French Equatorial Africa 1905, the western Maghreb, the Indian Ocean islands of Madagascar, Réunion, and Comoros, and Djibouti in the Horn of Africa. Within this African empire, territories in sub-Saharan Africa were treated primarily as colonies of exploitation.

Missionaries were among the earliest explorers of central and southern Africa. The London Missionary Society sent David Livingstone to South Africa in 1840, where he became one of the first Europeans to traverse the continent.

The British colonized Africa in about 1870. When they heard of Africa's valuable resources, such as gold, ivory, salt, and more, they did not hesitate to conquer the land. They wanted these resources because they needed them for manufacturing.

The missionaries, in their attempt to spread the Christian faith, win converts, and transform African societies, Christian missions of all denominations opened schools and disseminated education. Scientifically vital was their pioneer work in African languages. They were successful in translating the Bible into many African languages.

The missionaries of Africa also helped African societies advance in agriculture and technology, and in the process, they promoted a longer lifespan.

The African mythology, rich in artistic fables and true stories, offers a pantheon of gods and goddesses. Like Indian Brahma, Olorun (also known as Olodumare or Olofi) is the creator god who crafted the universe. Like Middle Eastern Baal, Chango is the god of thunder and storm. Although most Africans today are adherents of Christianity or Islam, African people often combine the practice of their traditional beliefs with the preparation of Abrahamic religions. The two Abrahamic religions are widespread across Africa, though primarily concentrated in different areas. **If so, actual African researchers can reveal more truth about Jesus Christ from which continent.**

The effects of missionaries on West Africa included a loss of cultural identity, a change in the unity of West Africa, an increase in nationalism, and a spread of Christianity due to trained black missionaries. There is no doubt that one of the benefits of missionary work for the African people is education and knowledge.

The colonialists plundered the natural resources on the one hand while the missionaries worked on the other. African colonization by the Europeans resulted in significant negative impacts on the economy, social and political system of African States. The most significant adverse effects of colonization were the exploitation of the natural resources by foreigners, which did not benefit the local communities but the colonizers.

OSHO: Indian Public Speaker - Rajneesh, also known as Acharya Rajneesh, Bhagwan Shri Rajneesh, and later as Osho, was an Indian godman, mystic, and founder of the Rajneesh movement. He was viewed as a controversial new religious movement leader and mystic. Let me quote one small story OSHO shared with his students.

Once a student asked a question:

Sir, The Jews are a tiny community, but from them came many prominent scientists, including Albert Einstein, thinkers, including Carl Max, who have emerged, and this small community has won battles with the Arabs; what is the reason.

OSHO replied:

Let me tell you about an incident; this is a true story. A conference I attended as the chief guest at an international school in the United States. It was a top-rated school for students from different countries; the Christian Church ran the school. There was also a ceremony to honor the best students of that school at the conference. When each child is called to give a gift, the teacher will provide a short explanation of their excellence. The last caller was a student who won first place in moral science.

His name was Jude; he was a Jewish boy. The teacher preached about his excellence; twelve students reached the final round of Moral Science. There were twenty-five questions, and both teams scored two points and drew. Finally, on the twenty-fifth question, the one who gives the correct answer to that question will win. I have asked the children.

- Who do you like and respect the most in the world?

The answers came from children, Abraham Lincoln, Mahatma Gandhi, Prophet Mohammad, Swami Vivekaanathan, Alexander the great, My Father, My Mother, etc.

Finally, it was Jude's turn; he said, Jesus Christ - As a Jew, he pronounces the name of Jesus; he was told that Jesus Christ was the one he respected the most. Jude, who answered the last question correctly, was declared the winner. When Jude received the prize, he received a standing ovation from the audience.

OSHO told me I felt something was wrong with this; none of the Jews I know respected or honored Jesus. They crucified Jesus Christ; they will do the same when Jesus comes again.

I asked, holding the child aside,

Why did you give such an answer?

He said with a smile, the ones I wear, respect, and love the most are Jehovah and Moses; Jesus Christ is the person I hate the most. But if you want a gift in this school, say the name of Jesus Christ.

These are Jews; they change tactics according to circumstances and time, which may not be suitable for beliefs and conscience. But it is often such people who succeed.

OSHO again continued,

There are also religious schools adjacent to Israeli schools, from 7 a.m. to 9 a.m. and then to 9 a.m.

They teach in a religious school that the earth is flat and that the stars move around the planet.

Once a child went to school after studying religion, and the science teacher asked if the earth was flat or round?

Without a doubt, he said the earth is flat.

Then the science teacher said it was until nine in the morning, after nine the earth is round, studying in a religious school must forget while looking in a science class. Thus, the Jew learned to see faith and science differently.

"While other nations are fighting each other over caste and religion, Israel and China are successfully pursuing their agenda."

What good is it for ordinary people will get to fight and die in the name of race and religion?

TO AFRICAN LEADERS AND THE CHILDREN OF AFRICA

The one raising the snake and protecting the terrorists will have to grieve simultaneously. Both of them will be obedient as long as they get their food and turn back if given a chance, leading to death. Terrorists never happen on their own, which is why some countries create terrorists for their ends. In countries with high poverty and hunger, young people and children are often the victims of terrorism. It is by sowing the seeds of caste and religion among such people that they are drawn into it. Terrorists can never be found in places where the Natural Reserve is not overcrowded, and there is no religious fight in those places. It is noted in Oil and Mineral-rich reserve countries in Africa and the Middle East that the terrorist plan is to make the people scared and spoil the economy so that oil will never come out.

- Al Shahaab Militant Group: Somalia, Kenya, Tanzania, Mozambique, Yemen

- Boko Haram: Niger, Chad, Nigeria, Mali, Cameroon
- Wilayah and Wilayat Wasat Ifriqiya : Central African Republic
- ISIL – Islamic State of Iraq and the Levant: IRAQ

And everyone knows about ISIS and Al Qaeda, their presence in the Middle East and worldwide.

Most of the latest weapons are reaching these terrorist groups. First, they are the ones advertising this weapon first by killing many people. All the children who know about these terrorist groups are illiterate and don't know how to read and write other than a few leaders controlling them. Therefore they cannot make any weapons with their technology.

Ordinary people and children may ask these questions.

- Who are the sponsors for these groups to purchase such expensive weapons?
- Who is feeding these many terrorist groups around the world?
- Each weapon the terrorist holding and using is manufactured in which country?
- Why do the United Nations or such organizations impose any embargo or sanctions against such manufacturers whose weapons reach the terrorist's hands out of their control? Such sanctions were imposed to protect a few white farmers in Zimbabwe because millions of people are under hunger and poverty in Zimbabwe. Even though those lands were colonized by the citizens of Zimbabwe and enslaved.
- Since these weapons are made from the Super Power countries, how come they reach without their knowledge? There can be a justification if a small number of firearms go their hand?
- Most terrorist groups are fighting to protect the religion in the name of God. Is there any God instructed anywhere in any holy books to go and kill innocent people and make them hungry forever and ever?
- Are these terrorists fighting to protect the people in those countries?

- If so, how many countries and their people have better lives because of terrorist activity?

The technology developed as simple as that can find even any metal parts though its frequency from any part of the world. Still, only the superpower countries cannot find the weapons the terrorist is hiding in front of the open book. Thanks to the weapon manufacturers and terrorists for protecting the world and the poor people.

This message for the leaders in such countries who are building and controlling the terrorists, if you believe a little compassion or goodness remains in your mind, fight against these atrocities to protect the world and the poor people from hunger and poverty. The African people are starving and sleeping on top of gold without knowing it. *We all know the terrorists are doing the terrorism and killing the people, not for GOD but to protect some countries' interest in selling their products and keeping those developing countries' assets not to coming out a remaining poor.*

We all know these terrorist groups and their activity are protecting to work for some colonialist interest and their benefits. It is a proven fact that no one will ever take any material assets to heaven or hell after the contract period of life on this earth—whether you are a millionaire, poor, black or white, or a terrorist. The only last right for all of us to go to the graveyard is a simple white cloth or a wooden box or little wooden pieces to burn; that is the only thing that comes along with you with the mercy of someone because we will never see which form, we are leaving of last day of our contract. **If you were, unfortunately, lying dead in a way no one could see, you would get a glass of water or a cloth to cover these poor people.**

Since the ancient Emperor Alexander to Steve Joe told the same

Alexander, after conquering many kingdoms, was returning home. On the way, he fell ill, and it took him to his death bed called his generals, and said. "I want the world to know the three lessons I have just learned.

Alexander took a deep breath and said:

"I will depart from this world soon; I have three wishes; please carry them out without fail."

1. "My first desire is that," said Alexander, "My physicians alone must" carry my coffin." - I want my physicians to have my coffin because people should realize that no doctor on this earth can cure anybody. They are powerless and cannot save a person from the clutches of death. So let not people take life for granted.

2. "Secondly, I desire that when my coffin is being carried to the grave, the path leading to the graveyard be strewn with gold, silver and precious stones which I have collected in my treasury"-I spent all my life Greed of Power, earning riches but cannot take anything with me. Let people realize that chasing wealth is a waste of time.

3. "My third and last wish is that both my hands be kept dangling out of my coffin"-I wish people to know that I came empty-handed into this world and empty-handed I go out of this world."

With these words, the king closed his eyes. Soon he let death conquer him and breathed his last. . . .

The billionaire "Steve Jobs" told the same person who passed away at 56 of Pancreatic Cancer. Net worth in September 2011 was US$ 7 Billion.

"These are his last words. I reached the pinnacle of success in the business world. "In others' eyes, my life is an epitome of success"

"However, aside from work, I have little Joy" In the end, wealth is only a cat of life that I am accustomed to. At this moment, lying on the sick bed and recalling my whole life, I realize that all the recognition and wealth I took so much pride in have paled and become meaningless in the face of impending death. You can employ someone to drive the car to make money for you. But you cannot have someone to bear the sickness for you. With time, we face the day when the curtain comes down".

Let us wait and see what colonial leaders from Africa or elsewhere in the world are going to say before they die:

Enough is enough!!!

For long years the United States and the permanent member states of the United Nations spent millions of dollars and efforts to make peace in Africa with the UN peacekeeping force.

How many countries have become peaceful in Africa with this investment in peacekeeping forces?

Who is making unrest in Africa other than the terrorist groups?

The colonial-funded terrorist is enjoying a significant share, and the weapon suppliers in Africa and France are looting the money from 14 countries; China is investing in Africa and trying to occupy the major projects for a long lease to build their business. **In effect, the UN peacekeeping force is there to support the colonialists in peacefully looting the assets from Africa, now known as peacekeeping.** In this context, the primary benefit is getting the service and support of the UN Peacekeeping force, especially for the colonialists, not Africa.

Former American President Donald Trump is an intelligent businessman; he aims to build America. In the Trump Administration, the United States generally has voted in the Security Council for the renewal and funding of existing U.N. peacekeeping operations, including those in

Africa. At the same time, the Administration has been critical of U.N. peacekeeping activities—both overall and in Africa specifically—and called for a review of operations to ensure that they are "fit for purpose" **(Trump Administration's assumption is correct – unfortunately, at present, the UN team in Africa is not fit for purpose including African Union Chair members- until 2020 October)** and to improve their efficiency and effectiveness. U.S. share of U.N. peacekeeping operation budgets at 27.89%; since the mid-1990s, Congress has capped the U.S. payment at 25% due to concerns that the current assessment is too high.

Over the years, Congress has considered a range of overarching policy issues and debates regarding U.N. peacekeeping operations in Africa, including,

- How effectively such operations fulfill their mandates, mainly related to civilian protection and peacekeeping;
- Under what circumstances a U.N. peacekeeping mission might be an effective tool for addressing or preventing mass atrocities in Africa
- To what extent and in what ways can U.N. peacekeeping operations effectively work with abusive or neglectful host governments and state security forces in Africa
- How to prevent and address sexual exploitation and abuse by U.N. peacekeepers, particularly in operations in Africa
- The role of Africa-led (as opposed to U.N.-conducted) operations as a response to regional crises.

HATS OFF TO Former PRESIDENT DONALD TRUMP for the review against UN Peacekeeping forces in Africa. No other presidents paid this much attention to supporting Africa, including Former President Baraka Obama, even though he was from the Black American community. It is because the COVID19 opened the eyes of the American government when American citizens lost their jobs and opportunities made the demonstrations against the US government to support their daily living. Imagine a small problem arising to shake the US government and that citizens become jobless and, in the street, protesting against the government and the governments are helpless to feed them since decades and decades African people are suffering from the same issues if you are the same category of human think of it how much of struggles African people going through the bad politics and colonialism.

May China be the next superpower?

European countries and the United States gave their technology to China just like they gave milk to the snakes. More than 60% of the products we see today are made in China, not just by China's intelligence or ability. It was as if the United States and Europe had given their technology to China for their temporary profit, so China acquired all the technology and became the world's manufacturing factory today. You may see every house and office on your table. More than 60% of the products will be manufactured in China. Looking at you and smiling, saying that I got you.

There is no doubt that China has succeeded in this game, thereby making China a prosperous country and spreading all over the world as a buying power with the money they made through this manufacturing game. China's vision is not for five or ten years but fifty or one hundred years. Before that, it was evident today that in every continent, strategic seaports were acquired for fifty or one hundred years when the loan obtained from China was not repaid. Jamaica to face the US, Sri Lanka to face India, Zambia to face Africa, and many more..... Thus, China's strategic advances and deployment continue. China grows, and its army grows and grows and spreads all over the world. China is moving continuously when other countries fight each other independently.

China is taught and helping all of us to wear the mask and use the Covid19 testing equipment, pre-manufactured from China before the release of Covid19, even though other countries have declared a lockdown, saying it is a mistake from China in the case of COVID19. China is doing more business than ever before, shutting down all trade around the world, spoiling all-economy around the world with just one virus, and the virus attack killing people around the world without using any investment to buy the weapons. This is an unspoken indication that China can control the whole world within a short time. No one can move anywhere because of the COVID19 restriction, but only China's products are moving worldwide faster than ever. In effect, all of the country's economy fell and struggled while China's economy grew. *Again, we must congratulate former President Donald Trump because, from the beginning, former President Trump keeps telling in a press conference that it is a Chinese virus.*

African leaders improved or not?

"The one who wants to get rich should give up the urge to borrow - in the same way, he who wants to gain power must give up his lust for power." But unfortunately, many of the African leaders work opposite and put their countries into debt.

A nation or an organization that protects the world does not need the poor people of Africa, but Europe, the United States, Japan, and China need elected leaders in Africa. Have these leaders been invited to their countries for half a century to better the poor people of Africa?

In that case, the ignorant would have to say that they were invited or that Africa and its people would not have been invited by their instructions. Why is Africa still starving if these countries are invited to improve Africa?

The need of these inviting countries is that Africa should never move better because if Africa is good, they will not be able to smuggle the raw materials they need from Africa at their discretion. The truth is that except for a few good leaders in Africa, other leaders are acting as if they do not understand the plundering of Africa. The only goal of these leaders is to live happily with their families to fill their bellies. In the living example, you can see that the children of African political leaders will be studying in Europe or America, have their investments, and live happily. However, the poor brothers and sisters of Africa still struggle for their daily living. Colonialists have a history of killing lead trying to tell the truth and d to develop Africa, so the truth may not come out. For example, more than 28 presidents have been killed in Africa in an attempt to build Africa.

There are several African summits happened and happening each year.

- African American summit
- African German summit
- African China summit
- African Japan summit
- African Russian summit

And so on…for never-ending summit…because Africa is the primary raw material resources for many ways, therefore every continent in the countries need Africa and its leaders to purchase them. It is always good to use the resources from its sources to make your life better. That may call it business. But don't forget the owners of the African land are also eligible to get their rights and allow them to eat their share. Not the 3-time full course meal, but at least one full meal a day.

"You can plug or steal the fruit as many you can get as far as the tree flourishes, but it is a request; don't cut the root."

One of the great leaders in Africa, DR. PLO Lumumba, is always shouting to African people to wake up; otherwise, these people will eat them alive, which has already been happening for a long time.

Do not expect any mercy from the colonialists; they are not inviting you to develop Africa; if so, how many technologies have been shared with African countries, and how many manufacturing companies have been built in Africa. They may make the roads, stadiums, buildings, bridges, Power plants, railways, and so on by getting the contracts favoring those countries and few political leaders in Africa. Unfortunately, none of the African diaspora's companies are not participating in these tenders and are not willing to take these tenders. They always complain about the African leaders and Africa while the countries walk away with big tenders and make millions and billions. But the colonial investors invested in building the infrastructure by providing heavy loans. Later, because of bad debt, those constructed areas will be pledged by the same colonialist by lack of no loan payments.

The main problem is that educated African people are not strong enough to oppose these to protect Africa. None of the African engineers are getting the opportunity to participate in these constructions or not getting the chance to prove their ability in Africa. Africa needs leaders like the forefathers who fought for freedom in Africa. After the release, the young generation is not strong enough to fulfill their dream of building Africa.

I want to tell you a story to illustrate my point. Once upon a time, a team of thieves planned to hunt in the African jungle using hidden weapons. For a few days, they didn't find anything other than small animals, and then they found a group of wild animals and their families.

In the same area, they discovered precious metals, but they could not enter those areas to take what they wanted because of the danger from the wild animals.

They started to attack the animals and killed as many as they could.

Among that group, one man decided to catch a pair of tigers, which he gave to a zoo. Then he and the other men started mining, looting the assets from Africa and taking those treasures to their homeland. At the zoo, the male tiger would not eat anything for a few days, and he tried his best to escape his cage. Each time he tried, he was struck a blow by the guards. The female tiger watched as her mate kept trying to escape but failed. Months passed, and along with the other animals, they learned to be obedient and eat what they were fed. A few months later, they had a baby tiger. This zoo was like a palace for him, and he began to enjoy himself with the other animals—he'd never.

Learned about hunting, for he had never been taught to hunt in the wild.

Again, the male tiger tried to escape but failed and was punished in front of his wife and son. One day the baby tiger asked, "Mama, why is my father trying to escape from us? We have food to eat and a place to sleep. Why is Papa like this?" The mother tiger explained the jungle, their freedom, and how much they enjoyed hunting in the wilderness. Just from listening to this, the male tiger's eyes were full of tears. At last, the tiger family decided to live peacefully, and together, they would play and do tricks for visitors.

A few years later, the zoo decided to sell the father tiger to a circus because he was obedient. He had forgotten life in the jungle and what it was like to be free. The thieves were still hunting in the wilderness. . . **and the young tiger had never taken any action to escape with his mother from captivity in the zoo.**

This is the real story of Africa now. The present generation has forgotten to resist—their teeth are no longer sharp, and they have forgotten how to hunt.

It is time for young people in Africa to wake up more vital than ever because you are wrong to think you can get everything only from the leaders. If you do not ask your right to meet your needs, your next generation will ask you what you did for Africa. Or when you leave this earth, your forefathers who fought for freedom will ask you what you did for your brothers and sisters.

They need to be able to take raw materials from Africa to other countries at legally reasonable prices. In return, Africa must get the technology to make new products in Africa using the same raw materials. If not, Africa will never improve. The main problem is that the African leaders, people in business, or educated people are not capable enough to bargain or negotiate with the people approaching the African government. Other countries demand raw materials from Africa, and when they come to Africa, they can order their needs in Africa, where there is no need to bow in front of them. Once your forefathers bowed down to their heads centuries ago and were eventually taken captive.

President of Ghana, Nana Akufo-Addo, is one of the great leaders who can roar like the grim lion in Africa in the 21st century. This leader has become a target in the eyes of the colonialists. What he has to say is boldly calling out to the world that this is not something those European countries, especially France, like at all. Also, we can count on a few more presidents like President of Tanzania John Magufuli, President of Rwanda Paul Kagame, and Hage Geingob.

President of Namibia, Mokgweetsi Masisi, President of Botswana. Many more Presidents in Africa are trying their best to develop Africa, but these said Presidents have already proven their signature in their country.

These Presidents are developing their countries similar to the copy of their forefathers who were ruled soon after the African independence in the 1960s. Those days the developments in Africa were excellent, and the African people's life was better than now. The products in infrastructure, educational institutions, health care systems, roads, and bridges are made during those days. The people from Asia and Europe had come to work for Africa. But after their power, the next generation of leaders, with the support of colonialists, again spoiled Africa. In effect, Africa got freedom, but Africa still did not bring space from the colonialist agenda, and still, the same colonialists-controlled Africa.

Africa is feeding all the continent, but Africa is still under hunger and poverty even though so many so-called nations demand that they support and provide for Africa. This is the opposite; if African wealth were not available to Europe, All the Europeans would die from hunger like those early days soon after World War.

The young generation of Africa must realize the truth that Africa is still prosperous; therefore, all the Europeans, Americans, Chinese, Indians, and Japanese still show the drama of love for Africa. Africa is a deep well that never runs dry. The onus is still on young people to keep that spring afloat.

Many times, Africans tried to unite together, but each time the European made sure that the Africans were within their control for their benefit.

The Lomé Convention is a trade and aid agreement between the European Economic Community (EEC) and 71 African, Caribbean, and Pacific (ACP) countries, first signed in February 1975 in Lomé, Togo.

In the Lagos Plan of Action in 1980, all the African countries decided to make their plan to build Africa with the Intra African trade. Still, the African Union did not show much interest in making it successful.

After being renewed three times, the Lomé Convention gave way in 2000 to the Cotonou Agreement, which made European aid compatible with the World Trade Organization and integrated the new priorities of the EU in the post-Cold War period.

Now the latest is the African Continental Free Trade Area is a free trade area that, as of 2018, includes 28 countries. The African Continental Free Trade Agreement created 54 of the 55 African Union nations. This is the continuation of Lagos's plan of action. The leaders realized that the colonialists would eat all the African raw without unity.

The Future vision of Africa 2063 is the continent's strategic framework that aims to deliver on its goal for inclusive and sustainable development and is a concrete manifestation of the pan-African drive for unity, self-determination, freedom, progress, and collective prosperity pursued under Pan-Africanism and African Renaissance.

All these agendas will be workable if the young generation and the diaspora worldwide can unite to support the present good African leaders. Colonialists are snatching wealth from Africa with the cheapness of food by adults who tell many stories from the hands of a small child. To stop this plunder, Africans need to prove to others that they are no more a child anymore.

CHAPTER ~ 7

THE LAST DAY OF MY ANCESTORS IN AFRICA

Make sure you will not cry by reading this page......Close your eye for 5 minutes if you are an African...or a humanitarian. Think of your Father and Mother, your grandparents, their father and mother, and their grandparents just for 4 or 5 generations back...you can see them on your own body, it's you four generations back because we are just a copy and memories of our ancestors.

Africa is the birthplace of humankind and knowing its history is essential for understanding the global society that's grown around it.

In the past, there was no distinction of race or color in Africa. Each had its tribes. It was about identifying them with each other, and each tribe had its boundaries. They clash and band together as a family, living happily like a mother's children.

The eldest of the family will rule as their leader. All family members respected him, and he says that's the law. They didn't even know what cheating was. Every mother is like a mother; all children are like their own children who live together. When a mother makes a meal, all the children go home and eat, all the children are equal to that mother, and it is the culture of Africa.

Some of the new children of the African diaspora never know who they are. It is the elder's responsibility to convey the previous stories to the young generation.

A Colonialist Father can offer the best toy for their daughters – Human enslaved person in a cage

Present black American and black European diaspora's ancestors reached not as a tourist where the place you live now. They were bound in chains and brought here as enslaved people without being given food to feed the dogs. Those who opposed were brutally executed, enslaved healthy young men and women were sold and taken into slavery to their land. The women fell victim to their sexual abuse; they took their children away from them.

The transatlantic slave trade began during the 15th century when Portugal and other European kingdoms were finally able to expand overseas and reach Africa. The Portuguese first started to kidnap people from the west coast of Africa and take those they enslaved back to Europe and America, followed by Arabs, Asians started getting involved in the slave trade business and exported to many parts of the world.

Zanzibar port was the leading destination for business tycoons. They brought the enslaved people from Somalia, Sudan, Kenya, Uganda, the Republic of Congo, Zambia, Malawi, etc. The primary Human slave selling point was named "STONE TOWN" – during those slavery times. Those who come to purchase enslaved women make sure she doesn't have sharpened teeth and a sexy body. The buyer can touch and check any parts of their body.

SLAVERS REVENGING THEIR LOSSES.

On the way to the final departure port:
Ghana, Zanzibar, Tanzania, or South Africa- The final departure zone:
"STONE TOWN" IN ZANZIBAR – TANZANIA IF YOU EVER VISIT ZANZIBAR, IT IS NEAR THE CRIST CHURCH, BUILT BY THE BRITISH.

In the book "Prisons & Slavery," John Dewar Gleissner writes: Published by Outskirts Press - "The Arabs' treatment of black Africans can aptly be termed an African Holocaust. Arabs killed more Africans in transit, especially when crossing the Sahara Desert, than Europeans and Americans, and over centuries, both before and after the Atlantic slave trade. Arab Muslims began extracting millions of enslaved Black Africans centuries before Christian nations did. Arab slave traders removed enslaved people from Africa for about 13 centuries, compared to three centuries of the Atlantic slave trade. Enslaved Africans transported by Arabs across the Sahara Desert died more often than enslaved people making the Middle Passage to the New World by ship. Enslaved people invariably died within five years if they worked in the Ottoman Empire's Sahara salt mines."

WOMEN SLAVE TRADE

Europeans, Americans, Arabs, and Asians have done nothing good for Africa except enslave African men, women, and children. Historian Kerala University Professor Jamal Mohammad, in his book *"History of Arab,"*- says female slaves captured in Europe were worth a thousand dinars, and female slaves from Turkey were valued at six hundred or more. Other enslaved Black women are valued depending on their energy and body structure.

A slave market in Khartoum, Sudan, c. 1876

19th-century engraving depicting an Arab slave-trading caravan transporting enslaved Black Africans across the Sahara.

Packing inside the Ship for Departure-Just think of their feeling of enslaved people.

The last day in Africa – enslaved people waiting to depart to the USA, Europe, or elsewhere.

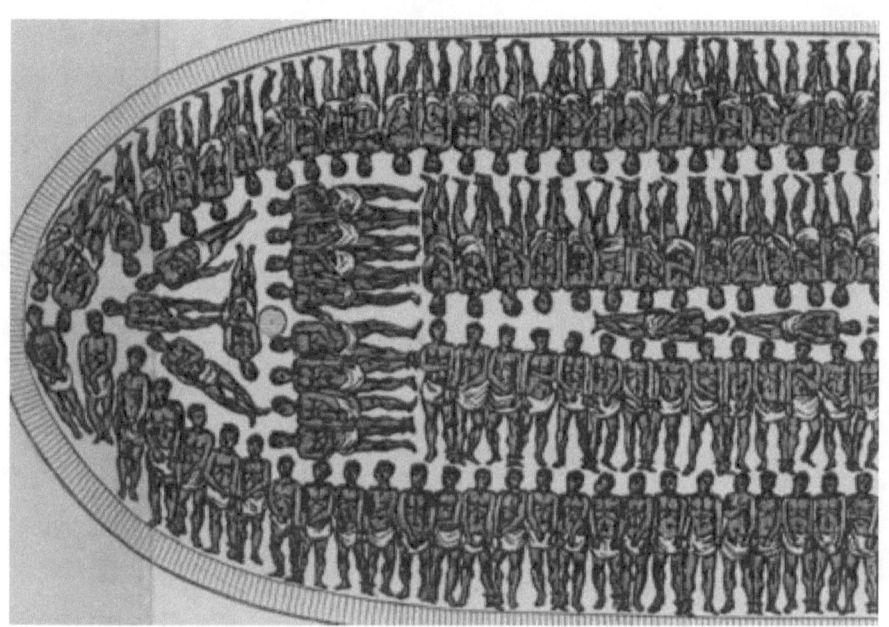

TERRIBLE PASSAGE FROM AFRICA TO AMERICA AND EUROPE BY SHIP.

Those enslaved shall sail their ship; they did work those even animals could not do. **The kings and queens queen of the African generation became enslaved and departed to too many countries.**

British colonialism ruled over Africa for centuries. They captured the most muscular men in the world as their slaves spread them into their territorial colonies to work their agricultural farms in America, Europe, and some parts of Asian Countries and sold the young African woman and mothers to some Arab countries.

Captured by slavers, they were marched along dirt tracks for 200 kilometers (125 miles) to slave castles perched on the Atlantic Coast, South Africa, or Ghana, where they boarded ships for North America or Europe. They never saw their homeland anymore…....

This may become some of your Grand – Grand Fathers??????

Until the 19th century, only the enslaved had suffered brutality because of human slavery. But ever since the whites learned that Africa was rich in natural wealth, slavery again started in different forms around the entire Africa.

These exiles no longer see their mother, family, or Africa. The tears of the men are still spread throughout the world. This continues today in many parts of Africa.

Now your ancestor's souls are waiting to receive you in Africa. You will never get a reward better than visiting your ancestor's land.

Have you heard of the world-famous Philosopher Plato?

Plato was an Athenian philosopher during the Classical period in Ancient Greece, the founder of the Platonist school of thought, and the Academy, the first institution of higher learning in the Western world.

After escaping from Athens and staying in Egypt for a while, Plato arrived in India while visiting other countries. He learned more from those masters and also exchanged his knowledge with the teachers at Nalanda Takshashila, one of the largest colleges in India at that time. He has shared this knowledge in his novels.

On his way, Plato saw and amazed by the vast elephants are tied to a small piece of wood.

What a fool you are? He asked the caretaker.

Don't you think the elephant will escape if these bushes are uprooted?

The caretaker of the elephant answered.

No, the elephant will never escape; it just turns around the wood. Plato was amazed at these words.

Again, the caretaker of the elephant explained,

When elephants are brought to the begging from the jungle, they are first chained to large chains, large trees, most substantial rocks, or concrete beams. At that time, the elephants will try to escape from it and fail; this will continue for a few days and forget again and again after it is clear and think that the elephant will not be able to escape. This helplessness will later become a habit. Once reached, the elephant never tries to run again. So, the elephant wanders around that little wooden stick.

Therefore, a tiny chain or a small stick is enough to restrain the elephants because the elephant believes that this is the same strong-most robust that cannot escape forever and will never try to break the chain or run again. This realization touched Plato so much that the lives of some humans and the lives of elephants were alike.

See, the love and care of African mothers even chuckled with the chain.

They are waiting for the owner to reach the final destination.

This is very similar to the life of the African people and the diaspora. Over the years, white colonialists enslaved the natives, and the African people learned to obey whites out of fear of being beaten and killed and obeyed. For more than five hundred years, this fear has not left them, and they still do not understand their strengths and that they have a better life than this. Those who once failed do not try to recover from the fear of failure again. Those who have made a habit of loss and grief will give up the thought of escaping. He will spend the rest of his life thinking that is his destiny. Only if this attitude changes the African people and the diaspora will survive. *Your forefathers were the generation that made even a lion tremble at a glance. It is the etiquette of Africa to respect those who should be respected, but why be afraid of others? That too from your own home.*

Many African leaders today have the same mindset. These leaders still fear the colonialists who ruled them before and the competition for power.

The will of the people must govern the government. Such good leaders are found in many African countries today in the 21ˢᵗ century, Such as:

- Professor Patrick Loch Otieno Lumumba- Kenya,
- Julius Malema- South Africa
- Joshua Maponga –Zimbabwe
- Rutendo Matinyarare -Zimbabwe
- Paul Kagame – Rwanda,
- John Magufuli- President of Tanzania,
- Muhammadu Buhari- President of Nigeria,
- Nana Addo Dankwa Akufo-Addo - President of Ghana,
- Adama Barro – President of Gambia,
- Danny Faure – President of Seychelles,
- Roch Marc Christian Kabore – President of Burkina Faso,
- George Weah – President of Liberia,
- Joao Manel Laurenco _ President of Angola,
- Macky Sall – President of Senegal,
- Sahle Work Zewde – President Ethiopia,
- Cyril Ramaphosa – President of South Africa and many more.

The natural leader is the one who rules the country with zeal for the goodness of the country. But if the authorities become dictators, the government will perish. The leaders of each country should introspect themselves from time to time and avoid self-government if they are convinced they cannot govern properly. Such positions must be handed over to the leader who can rule the country. **"It is better to stop the song when the tone is good."**

"IF YOU CAN THINK ABOUT WHAT YOU WANT IN YOUR MIND. AND MAKE THAT YOUR DOMINANT THOUGHT YOU WILL BRING IT into YOUR LIFE:" by Plato.

Yes, this is the time all African diaspora must think about what they want in their life; it's time for them to think about their own country, Africa. If your goal in Africa is good, then your leaders are open way to you, don't be late.

A message to the young African diaspora:

"Your life is not about going to bed after having a few drugs or alcohol and eating a burger. Do not forget that you are the generation that needs to lead Africa better."

The world is under the competition of sending rockets, satellites, and humans to send to Moon and Mars or some other planet. I want to say to the African diaspora, let them find their ancestors are staying on the moon or Mars or some other planets. You know your ancestors are from African Continent kidnaped by white colonialists by force and killed or thrown to either to the animals or the Mediterranean Sea the minor children, older adults which they believed no use for them, the rest of them reached to work enslaved people brought to America or some other parts of the world.

It is your responsibility to find your ancestors, yes, your DNA, who are still struggling with those same colonialists in the new style of colonialism. The saddest part is that some of the bad politicians are worse than "hyenas" (hyena is one of the animals in the forest that kill and eat their brothers and sisters or father or mother when they get the chance while there is nothing else to eat) within Africa still supporting to the white colonialist especially to France (All other countries except France like a dog smelled the bone, still don't want to stop their direct colonization in Africa and no countries including United Nations or African Union are Questioning to France for this brutality against Africa) to spoil the African continent.

Many African Americans and European Africans are on the Millionaires and Billionaires list. If you believe t your DNA is natural, as an African diaspora, the first step is going to Africa and doing part of your investment o support your brothers and sisters. That's how you prove yourself that your lineage from the African continent. The question is, from which part of Africa? No problem, when the colonialists kidnaped your ancestors from the African continent, it was just known as "Alkebulan," which means Mother of Mankind which is the present African continent. After that lot of invasion and colonization brought different names divided into 55 countries; again, the colonialists tried to divide those 55 countries into many countries to fight each other and kill themselves so that they could quickly loot the African assets for their own countries.

Because of your absence, all other countries like Chinese, Europeans, Americans, and Asians are investing in Africa, and these business people are not giving any high positions to Africans. In effect, Africans are still enslaved. Your investment can save Africa and African descent.

Just close your eyes for a moment and recap those seen when they were caught by the colonialists and killed or thrown out the babies, grandmothers, and fathers. The scene where the happily suckling babies are snatched out of the mothers and thrown away when that baby is crying where the place they dropped when that mother and father are taken hostage while the babies are crying outside. Your forefathers or mothers may be one among them who brought from that brutality and reached to the countries where you live now as enslaved people or partial enslaved people. Can you imagine it was you as a father or a child then? I can't even think of it. So, imagine the pain they had gone through after arrival and worked as enslaved people for many centuries. Their souls are crying to reach out to your brothers and sisters and help them.

You must go to the place back in Africa where your ancestors were taken captive and sent on their journey and name that place "the Gate of Heaven." Spend some of your savings for that as a charity to remember your ancestors. Let those souls of your ancestors rest in Peace.

The record shows at least the following numbers of indigenous ancestry in the American Continent.

10 Million Enslaved Africans were brought to the Americans

4 Million sent to the Caribbean's

1.5 Million were sold in the British West indies

And to different Islands like Dominica, Grenada, Jamaica, St. Lucia, St. Kitts, St. Vincent, St. Thomas, Trinidad, Pan Caribbean, Cauca Valley, Colombia, Uruguay, and many more…

Unless otherwise you, the African diaspora, do not come to Africa; the continent of Africa will never be free from the colonizers. If you are not asking the world, then who is the one to be there to support your brothers and sisters in Africa?

The white colonialists were looting all the assets from Africa, and France had been stealing direct cash from 14 countries until now. Even United Nations is not questioning that because you as a diaspora are not shouting for that. France is still colonizing with their power insisting to Africa that the Francophone countries must buy weapons from France and the weapons coming to those countries legally and illegally. It would help if you thought about how the children and terrorist groups like AL-QAEDA, AL SHABAB, BOKO HARAM, and LORDS RESISTANCE ARMY. They are only a few thousand in number. But they carry the latest weapons; how do these groups get weapons? Who is paying for that? It is none other than the colonialists controlling Africa with the support of some bad African leaders for their benefit. What is United Nations doing for that? You, as a diaspora, must come out from your comfort and take ownership to save Africa.

Mama Arikana asks the questions to the African diaspora:

- Why is it so difficult for Africans to say enough is enough?
- How long will we watch this carnage go on, and we say nothing?

Mama says it goes back to our mind, it goes back to our fear, and it goes back to that inferiority. Until we, the black people, understand that we are suffering from the legacy of colonization that was suffering from the estate of slavery, then we all make the chuckles of the thought the chuckles of our feet and hands are freed, the chuckles of our minds continue. Until we realize that we are wounded people and need healing, nothing in our circumstances will change.

In effect, Africa is still not free, under the feet of the former colonizers. African diaspora must wake up, wake up with the power of a lion, sharpen your teeth like a tiger, run like a cheetah to Africa, remove your old feathers like an eagle to fly high, go to Africa and hunt those colonizers and make them as your slaves by proving your strength and developing Africa, let the colonizers come and beg you for their meal because Africa is the source of Humankind and is a significant asset holder in the world until today.

"Where love reigns, the impossible may be attained."

WELCOME HOME

"African diaspora's – welcome to the new world of Africa."

Your Forefathers and freedom fighters sacrificed their lives to be free from colonialists. But Africa could not escape the plunder of the colonialists. For over fifty years, some of the worst leaders in Africa have supported these colonialists. Many leaders have realized this and are working day and night to save Africa. Now, these leaders and Africa need your support, especially your experience, Knowledge, and financial and moral strength.

The only way Africa can come up is through industrialization within Africa. Automation refers to manufacturing products within Africa, both domestic and international, from the raw materials currently being exported. Through this, jobs for the African diaspora worldwide and people in Africa can be replaced by living standards and poverty.

Although the DNA of Africa is spread all over the world, see the figures from the following ten countries:

Few numbers of African Diaspora (DNA) around the world.

- Peru: 1.2 Million
- Mexico 1.3 Million
- United Kingdom: 2 Million
- Jamaica: 2.7 Million

- Venezuela: 3.4 Million
- France: 5 Million
- Colombia: 5.3 Million
- Haiti: 11 Million
- United States of America: 46.3 Million
- Brazil: 83.2 Million

Wouldn't the ten percent of Africans in these countries be in the big business, and Africa would survive if their network of companies expanded to Africa????........???

IS AFRICA SAFE TO DO BUSINESS FOR THE AFRICAN DIASPORA?

The main question mark for all the Afro American and the African diaspora around the world is whether Africa is safe?

Yes, Africa is safe to settle and do business after all the African countries independence. But it was the colonialist agenda again to scare the people worldwide. The prominent former European colonialists set this plan; Germany, France, Belgium, British, and Portugal played a significant role. Africa colonization began in the 17th century; the Netherlands started exploring and colonizing Africa. While the Dutch were waging a long war of independence against Spain, Portugal had temporarily united with Spain, starting in 1580 and ending in 1640.

All Africans and the African diaspora must study the Belin conference to learn about the agenda of the colonialists that how to control Africa for centuries and until now in the 21st century.

Berlin Conference in 1884 determined how to break up Africa into colonies for their respective countries. At a conference in Berlin, held from November 1884 to February 1885, Chancellor Bismarck organized the meeting to lay down the rules that should govern the colonization of Africa and how to settle European countries would claim colonial land in Africa and avoid a war among European nations over African territory. The Berlin Conference spanned almost four months of deliberations, from 15 November 1884 to 26 February 1885. By the end of the Conference, the European powers had neatly divided

Africa up amongst themselves, drawing the boundaries of Africa much as we know them today. Before European colonialism, it is estimated that Africa had up to 10,000 different states and autonomous groups with distinct languages and customs. From the mid-7th century, the Arab slave trade saw Muslim Arabs enslave Africans.

The Berlin conference included 13 European powers and the United States. They were Austria- Hungary, Belgium, Denmark, France, Germany, Italy, the Netherlands, Ottoman Empire, Portugal, Russia, Spain, Sweden- Norway, the United Kingdom, and the United States.

The Berlin Conference led to a period of heightened colonial activity by the European powers. Except for Ethiopia and Liberia, all the states that make up present-day Africa were parceled among the colonial powers within a few years after the meeting.

Imperialist ambitions in Africa were boosted by the expansion of competitive trade in Europe. ... The rapid growth of industries made European countries look to Africa for a supply of cheap raw materials and (enslaved person) labor. West Africa was essential for the development of industries in Europe. Thus, they enslaved the African people plundering all of Africa's territories and mineral assets like gold, copper, cobalt, uranium, diamonds, and antiquities. You can see the centuries-old antiques in all the European Museums.

Africa was the hunting land for the Europeans; developing Europe and their family's wealth was the only plan for the colonialist. Whoever tried to open their mouth against colonialism was brutally killed. They took all the raw materials from Africa, used the same African people as their slaves, and took out Africa for their colonized countries other than the African Continent. From 1885 to 1920, colonialists killed over 10 million African people. At least 8 million people were exported from Africa to different continents, including Asia, and over 8 million people were enslaved within Africa and over 35 countries under the colonialist umbrella. This enslaved generation of over 170 million people living out of Africa as African Diasporas.

ALKEBULAN

"The ancient name of Africa was Alkebulan. Alkebu-lan is the "mother of mankind" or "garden of Eden." Alkebulan is the oldest and the only word of indigenous origin. It was used by the Moors, Nubians, Numidians, Khart-Haddans, and Ethiopians.

The name mother of humanity welcomed European into Africa like her own children, but the Europeans colonized that mother itself as a reward to that mother. That was the only mistake that happened to African mothers. From that day onwards, they spend a considerable amount of money on advertising to the world that Africa is not safe, African leaders are brutal, and Africa is poor. And Europeans various organizations played a significant role in advertising this propaganda.

Their aim is for the other countries not to look into Africa while they loot the raw materials from Africa. In front of the world, Europe is the only one providing AID, food packages, medicine, etc. Still, such a developing country holds the latest weapons all over the villages, especially near the mining areas. From where these weapons are coming, go and check these weapons are made by which country. These weapons are making noise every day to make scare the people. But other than this mining area, all the African countries are safe.

Africa is the authentic Garden of Eden…. All the African diaspora must come home.

I want to ask you these points to think about…

- If Africa is not safe, why have all the European companies been there for centuries, doing billions of businesses and looting the assets?
- If Africa is a dangerous place, how come the Chinese colonized almost all the African countries doing business freely and importing all their manufactured items to Africa?
- How many Chinese businesspeople were killed because of bad African people or government?
- Some 67 million tourists visited Africa in 2018, representing a rise of 7% from a year earlier, making Africa the second-fastest-growing region when it comes to tourism, after the Asia Pacific,

- How many tourists were killed because of bad African people or leaders?
- If Africa is not safe, then why do Tourists in Africa come mainly from Asia, Europe, and the US. France is the number one source, followed by the UK and the US.
- How many Europeans or American tourists were killed in Africa because of bad African people?

None...........................until now.

The fact is that Former Ugandan President Idi Amin Dada's movie may have been made to scare the people around the world into believing that Africa is not safe. That was the mistake of the Former Ugandan President, but Africa no longer exists. Who knows that was the real story?

MANUFACTURING OPPORTUNITIES IN AFRICA

No need to tell anyone that Africa is rich in natural resources. It is enough to manufacture only the goods that Africa needs. With the success of the African Free Trade, it will be easier to deliver manufactured goods to all countries within the African Continent. This will reduce imports to Africa and thereby increase Africa's economy.

"The first thing a hungry person needs are food, not the Word of God, If he gets enough food for his body, he will be ready to listen to the word of God."

The goal must be to cultivate the food that Africa needs. The soil in Africa is so fertile that it only needs water to grow. Rivers, streams, and lakes kiss and greet Africa and warmly welcome farmers. The African diaspora interested in agriculture will only need little money to purchase a few seeds and tools to sow.

Leaders in many African countries are promoting agriculture. Many countries have granted exemptions from agricultural equipment import duty.

Tanzania has an excess of 25 million tons of food production a year, President John Magufuli has recently announced, and Tanzania is ready to export within the African continent to support the African People. From 2005 onwards, Tanzania moved in the right direction of development. It is attracting the investors through the government partnership and private sector and arranging all the infrastructure, Road highways, Railways, Shipyard, etc. Julius Nyerere Hydropower Station, also called Rufiji Hydroelectric Power Station, is a 2,115 megawatts hydroelectric dam under construction in Tanzania. The power station is expected to produce 5,920Giga Watts of power annually. It will solve the entire power problem for Tanzania, and hopefully, the excess energy can be supplied to the nearest countries.

Visit: YouTube: Julius Nyerere Hydropower Station: The Century's Biggest Turnkey Project in Tanzania

President Paul Kagame of Rwanda builds poverty into food safety and education. Rwanda has become one of the cleanest cities in Africa. Other Presidents can copy this hygiene because;

"The first impression is the best impression" shows who you are. Imagine in a seven-star buffet lunch or dinner you have 25 high-class dishes on the menu and that in front you are keeping a piece of shit in the natural color and smell then who will eat that food? So, the waste disposal management system must be the first step in any country.

The ideas President's strategy of Geographic Centrality, Political Stability, and Ease of doing business brought the investors to Rwanda. Paul Kagame proves through action rather than wasting time speaking for the country's upliftment. The investors can apply for the trade license through an online portal and the permit within the same day to start their own business. Through this, Rwanda has become the best President of Rwanda who cannot replace the country from the hearts of the Rwandan people.

Some other African country's Presidents are also focusing on building their counties on their level best to remove the corrupted leaders and bring prosperity to the African continent. These leaders know without removing corrupted leaders, Africa will never be free from under the umbrella of the colonizers.

Following are the excellent leaders trying their level best to develop their countries.

- Nana Addo Dankwa Akufo-Addo - President of Ghana
- Hage Geingob - President of Namibia
- Adama Barro – President of Gambia
- Danny Faure – President of Seychelles
- Roch Marc Christian Kabore – President of Burkina Faso
- George Weah – President of Liberia
- Joao Manel Laurenco _ President of Angola
- Macky Sall – President of Senegal
- Sahle Work Zewde – President Ethiopia
- Cyril Ramaphosa – President of South Africa

Sudan: Although there is still some political instability, the Agricultural sector is improving very well. Whichever party comes into power, all are promoting the food production area. Import duty has been wholly abolished in Sudan, where farmers have started large-scale farming. In a brief period, Sudan will achieve complete food security. The United States of America and Israel recently made the joint venture agricultural proposal to the Sudanese Government; it will be an excellent strategic move if this plan comes true. Still, Sudan Government must ensure that the Sudanese government will be getting their share equally, unlike in the early days of colonial ideas of not giving anything to the people's government. Also, it will be a good idea that at least 50% of production must sell within the country to protect the food safety of the Sudanese people. The saddest part is the African diaspora does not recognize the potential of Africa, and they are still not reaching Africa for business.

Sebastian Joseph invested in this Organic Onion, Vegetable, and Sheep farm with Sudanese partners Suleiman El Mehadi and El Hadi Abdulrahman Mohammad Ahmad.

Solarized farm.

Sudan Onion Farm   Sudan Carrot Farm

Sudan Sheep Farm Investment from Sebastian
Joseph to support African Farmers

In areas with no rivers in Sudan, cultivation is done using solar power for water irrigation for the agricultural sector.

As said earlier, Africa is the mainland of all the natural resources.

Minerals and Precious Stones.
Diamond/Kimberlite, Platinum, Gold, Silver, Copper, Iron, etc.,

The African continent is blessed with rich in Minerals; 80% of the world's minerals are minted from African Continent.

Following are some of the countries.

- Botswana: Diamond/Kimberlite, Gold, Silver, Copper, Precious Stones.
- South Africa: Diamond/Kimberlite, Gold
- Somalia: Gold, Copper, Iron
- Nigeria: Gold, Copper, Iron
- Sudan: Gold, Precious Stones
- Egypt: Gold, Copper, Precious Stones
- Tanzania: Gold, Copper, Precious stones
- Burundi: Gold, Copper,
- Mali: Gold, Copper, Precious Stones.
- Central African Republic: Gold, Copper, Cobalt, Uranium
- And many more.....................

Tantalum is found only in Africa, and few quantities are located in China. Tantalum is used in the electronics industry for capacitors and high-power resistors. It is also used to make alloys to increase strength, flexibility, and corrosion resistance. The metal is used in dental and surgical instruments and implants. Chinese people mining Tantalum from Africa and keeping this product are their monopoly.

Gold Mining: Almost all African countries have a gold reserve; Ghana is one of Africa's best places to look for gold. It is one of the continent's top gold-producing countries and supports several large gold companies. Mali, Burkina Faso, Sudan, Tanzania, and Burundi are also looking for investors to partner with the Government for exploration and Mining.

Like it or not, Africa is now tremendously developing its GDP rate @ 6 to 9 percent yearly, which means the manufacturing opportunities are very high. When the countries develop means, the infrastructure materials are very much required, and almost all the items can be produced within African resources.

- Steel Manufacturing Company: Iron and scrap are available in most African countries; there are not many manufacturing plants in each country. Unfortunately, Africa is importing over 80% of the steel from other countries even though Africa is exporting iron ore to other countries, including China, for building homes, roads, Stadiums, and all steel-related productions are essential when a country is in the development stage. Here the investors can think of opening a steel factory. So far, there are no vehicle manufacturing plants in Africa. The huge Iron reserve will open the opportunities to produce Ship Manufacturing ships within Africa.

- Uranium is essential because it provides us with nuclear fuel to generate electricity in nuclear power stations. It is also the primary material from which other synthetic trans uranium elements are made. Uranium is the primary raw material for making all kinds of nuclear and other related weapons; this is why, over centuries, Germany, Britain, France, Italy, and Belgium colonized and brutally killed many of the people in Africa, and they are the most prominent weapon manufacturers in the world. 90% of them are going from Africa. Uranium can be used to produce power stations and other good causes for the African people.

- Copper Manufacturing: Central Africa and Congo is the primary source of copper; they can be found in many other African countries. Until now, the colonial mafia produced millions of tons of Gold Copper and its byproducts of Cobalt; cobalt is the primary raw material for producing all kinds of batteries. Without a coper, even gold jewelry, computer Processer, Memories, electronics panel boards, etc., cannot make. Without coper and batteries, no world and no mobile phones. The copper manufacturing companies can plan copper cables and related products. These are just a few......

These countries are producing billions of dollars worth of Gold, Copper, and Uranium, but unfortunately, people are struggling for their daily bread in these countries. Who is responsible?

United Nations peacekeeping force has been there for many years with their military and vehicle, but for what?????

To support the people's wealth or protect the colonialists exploiting the minerals from these countries?????

Just google "Central African Republic exploitation YouTube," and you will know a clear picture of these countries and their potential. Each year we hear the news from the media that the United Nations spends half-billion or one billion dollars to support African people. Not even 10% of the money is not reaching Africa. But they are bringing only a few foods and medicine items as AID supplies to these countries. But how many billions of weapons have been imported to this country, and how many billions of Gold, copper, and other minerals exploiting by these countries? That news is not brought in front of the world or not preventing the import of weapons nor not stopping the exploitation. Then what is the use of these peacekeeping forces over there????? Religion plays a significant role here, both the Christians and Muslims, to protect God, not the people. Again, who are you to protect GOD? GOD knows how to defend himself. You save yourself and your family. Are you the savior of GOD?

"The Congo River can produce the Electricity and drinking water for the entire African continent, but because of the colonial rule until 21st century this project is not initiated by purpose" A Group of African diaspora can think of it to develop the Hydro energy power plant in Congo. You have to come with your American passport as American Citizen to grow the business first; then, only the other European colonialists presently stationed in Congo will move out from there.

Those are just a few examples of the manufacturing opportunities with the raw materials.

Agricultural production:

Ghana is the mother of tomatoes. Unfortunately, even the tomatoes are also imported from Italy and China. China is producing and exporting 16 million tons per month, double the quantity of Italy. Most of these productions are coming to Africa. Ghana's Government is not paying much attention to this industry; the reason can be importers' mafia or lack of knowledge? The same problem for Rice is that rice is imported from Thailand to Ghana, although Ghana can produce the rice for the whole African continent. But Ghana imports rice for over 500 million dollars every year.

Cattle meat and milk products can also be produced in Africa. This is just a matter of coordination and a few investments, either from the Governments or the African diaspora around the world. If you don't wake up now, your children and grandchildren will curse you if you don't take this opportunity. It is so bad that all the domestic products are imported from China, India, Thailand, and European countries even though Africa is blessed with good weather, seasonal rains, fertile soil, and the river flowing around Africa. This is the apparent mistake of the leaders in each African country. Those not focusing on these areas spend a little to remove African people's poverty. Investing in Agriculture eliminates the hunger of the poor people, reducing imports and increasing exports. This can bring the GDP level up for each African country. These imports are declining the job opportunity for African people and growing poverty. Who is responsible??????

Former President John Magufuli of Tanzania clearly stated that, and it is true – "No uncles or Aunts or brothers will never come to protect you if they are coming it is for their benefits only not for African people" President Magufuli is correct because that is what the history of Africa proven for the past five centuries.

Investing a little money in a tomato manufacturing/processing plant can serve the whole of Africa. The farmers are facing the challenge of seasonal rain and water. A small solar water pump can solve this for most farms. The Sudanese government supports the farmers with Solar Technologies. To start a tomato plantation, you require less than

$5 000/- if you can borrow the land from the farmer or associate with farmers with the partnership.

Cocoa is produced in Ghana and exported to Switzerland, the UK, and other parts of Europe to make chocolates and imported back to African countries. Many Ghanaians do not know the use or taste of chocolate; they know how to farm and sell cocoa. Opening the chocolate manufacturing plant and exporting from Africa can make millions of dollars in profit and job opportunities for the people within the countries. **If the Ghanaian Government can add 5% more in export duty for coco, all other agricultural activity in Ghana will be alive and well. Because of this 5%, no European countries will reject this coco because it is unavailable.**

THIS POLICY HAS BEEN ADAPTED ALREADY IN TANZANIA BY PRESIDENT JOHN MAGUFULI AND RWANDAN PRESIDENT PAUL KAGAME. I wish all the presidents of entire Africa do the same to remove their people from hunger and poverty.

Cashew nuts: Tanzania, Uganda, Rwanda, Burundi, Senegal, Zambia, Zimbabwe, and many African countries produce Cashews, but it is exported with or without processing and comes back to Africa in beautiful packing from Europe and all other continents. Opening the Cashew nut processing plant is another opportunity.

Potatoes: All the 55 Countries in Africa can produce Potatoes, but the potato chips are imported. This is a massive opportunity for the African diaspora thinking of small business, but it can give big profit. Even the onion is importing most African Countries. What is missing is little money for plantation and support. These are the most significant opportunities awaiting the African diaspora around the world. The described products are just a few; you think what you want to do, all the raw materials are available in Africa that is the beauty of Africa.

Remember: As an American or European diaspora, you can save many young people's life by investing a little bit in African Countries. **A recent study shows more than 2000 migrants died in 2018 alone attempting to reach Europe via the Mediterranean Sea and many hundreds of deaths in the Sahara Desert in recent years on the way to searching for jobs to protect their families.**

Many of them are arrested and are in the Libyan Jail like slaves without food or proper accommodation, caught by the Libyan authorities on the way trying to pass the Sahara Desert to Europe. But the European Union also did not take any action to save them. It is your responsibility because they are from your DNA.

Indeed, one day, we all have to leave this earth; life is a journey. But before we leave this earth, you must put a signature on the planet. That signature can be your assigned mission to protect your family and other people struggling in the world, especially in Africa. Putting a lot of money in the bank account and showing the world that I am a millionaire can give joy only to your mind. No one will enjoy or share that joy, and that signature will never sustain in the world forever. But opening the opportunities for too many people to get their job to fill their bellies would be the most significant thing. That signature will sustain for generation and generation. Let that signature be in Africa before you leave the earth.

Make a trip to Africa to the place you believe that your ancestors or friends, it is guaranteed that you will never want to go back to USA or Europe again. Because once you reach your mother country, there will be no color difference; you will be one among them except South Africa. South Africa still has black and white problems exists.

"A lesson for all of us is that for every loss, there is victory, for every sadness, there is joy, and when you think you have lost everything, there is hope" - By Plato.

If you believe that you have only a little money as your savings and plan to settle in any country, Africa is the best choice because with the small capital in a rich country, you are still poor, but with that bit of money in developing countries, you will be rich. The choice is yours; in Africa, no one will call you **"HEY BLACK MAN."** Many black Americans have already started moving to Ghana, Kenya, Tanzania, Gambia, and many more. **Next, maybe you????** The mother of Africa is waiting for you. So, you, too, can sleep on the African soil where the souls of your ancestors end up listening to the song of that Grandparents.

For your information, many African Americans visit Ghana and receive the traditional names, like new baptism in Ghana. Even the American Comedian and Motivator **Steve Harvey** visited Ghana and many other countries. After seeing the enslaved person trade castle about his ancestors who came through that last destination to the USA as enslaved people, he expressed his sentimental words.

Steve Harvey quoted: "My grandfather and their ancestors were the enslaved people in America until abolishing the slavery in the USA. Other nationalities like British, Polish, German, Asian, etc., living in America have their own country. But we black African Americans have no country to name it other than Africa because our ancestors were enslaved by the colonialist from which African country we don't know" he is recommending all the African Americans must visit Africa, the white propaganda we hear through the media is not valid.

Prof. PLO Lumumba and Dr. Arikana Chihombori Quao, along with other members on the recent zoom meeting with Make Afrika Great channel advising the African diaspora.

"The time is now for you to liberate yourself from that chain chuckled off low self-esteem and recognize wherever you are…. your home is best."

You are out there in the United States of America, Europe, or other parts of the world; there is a sense that speaking metaphorically, and you must now come home. You can contribute much to Africa; we want to invite you to invest in the banking sector. Why should the Irish, Americans, and Japanese invest in the African Development Bank? Why can't the African diaspora can invest in the African Development Bank? Can't we not? Let us go into the area of Agriculture; who is propagating our seeds? Are you safe if somebody is responsible for bearing the roots to feed yourself? Can't you invest in Agriculture? Can't we invest in pharmaceuticals? Why is it Johnson and Johnson and Roach? Can't we invest in that area? And the many places you can invest – Professor PLO Lumumba is asking these questions to the African diaspora. This is the time to come together.

The word of Julius Kambarage Nyerere, "IT CAN BE DONE LET US PAY OUR PART," can be done. Let us play our part. The diaspora has a role to play and a fundamental role. Your journey starts from now……. To save many lives.

"He who does not travel does not know the value of men."

CHAPTER ~ 9

CORRUPTION IS A MATTER FOR THE AFRICAN DIASPORA?

For whatever a man will have sown, that also shall he reap. For whoever sows in his flesh shall also reap corruption from the meat. But whoever planted in the spirit, from the sprite, he shall era eternal life. (Holy Bible-Galatians 6:8)

- Can pumpkin germinate if paddy seeds are sown?
- Will the falcon hatch from the hen's egg?
- Will the lamb gives birth to the tiger?

Therefore, if a child is born of a father who is a thief, do not expect anything good from him except theft. The legacy of the colonialists is the same; only certain infectious diseases or their bombs can change them. Even God will not change them because God will require some devils to compare God and devils.

"If you gain the whole world and lose your soul, what good is it?"

Corruption is common in most countries in the world. There are good and bad leaders; it all depends on how they are nurtured from childhood and will continue until their death. Few people are changing in between when they realize that real-life mean not making more money through illegal source.

"To move the world, we must first move" – By Socrates.

It is the habit of some to find fault with others to cover up their incompetence. Such people keep talking about corruption and the negative news in that country. Those who want to better themselves or want the government to be better off do not make such accusations. They will fight against it, and none of this applies to the business people. Leaders of all African countries are who make all the arrangements for investors in Africa. Yes, in some countries, some leaders may steal a little that will be projected to the media as to massive corruption. But in the meantime, the colonialists are looting billions of dollars from that country. No media will talk about it with giant advertisements. Again, this is also a part of the colonialist plan to project the leaders in front of the people and the world so that the attention will turn to the leaders only, not the colonialists.

KHOW THYSELF - By Socrates: - "We can work miracles if we recognize ourselves and are willing to change ourselves."

Some of you might read about this story.

A shoemaker goes to a blanket seller's shop with the money he has saved to buy a blanket to escape the winter cold. But he refused to give the blanket because he did not have enough money. In that frustration, the shoemaker went to the bar and drank. On his way home, he saw a man sleeping in front of the church chapel without a dress on that winder at night. Out of fear, the shoemaker did not approach the young man. He walked home, but a question arose in his mind, He may sometimes die of cold and starvation. He told himself young man is not going to rob me, nor I don't have anything to lose. The shoemaker approached the young man, took off his coat, handed it to him, and took him along with him to his own house.

The Shoemaker's wife, who was waiting for her husband to come with a blanket, saw her husband coming with another poor man being picked up without a blanket. She got angry with her husband and shouted at him. Only a little bread can survive for two days for us; I am not going to serve the food for any other man, she shouted to her husband. The Shoemaker and the young man who came with him said nothing. But after a few moments, she felt sorry for the young man and thought that sometimes he was good and had not eaten for days. She started making soup and served it along with the bread for him. The young man looked at her and smiled.

The young man decided to stay in the same house and quickly started learning to make the shoe from a shoemaker. The whole village became aware of the uniqueness of the shoes he made.

Once, a wealthy man came to the shoemaker with expensive leather and told him that these were very expensive leathers brought from Germany to make beautiful shoes for me. If you make any mistake, you will be in jail; he told the shoemaker. These words frightened the shoemaker and entrusted the young man to make the shoe. The young man looked at the rich man a smiled, but seeing the young man laughing, Rich Man said, "If the shoes are not good, your laughter will end." And he went.

But when he saw the young man making sandals instead of a shoe, the shoemaker thought himself again, "Should I go to jail because of him?"

The early morning the next day, somebody knocked on the door; the shoemaker opened the door, saw a rich man's servant in front of him, and told the shoemaker. I came on the orders of the rich man's wife. The rich man no longer needs shoes because the rich man died on the way home from here. All he needs is a pair of sandals for the dead. The shoemaker looked at the young man surprisingly. The shoemaker gave the sandals to that servant man.

After a few days, a woman and two girls approached the shoemaker to make the shoes for that girl; they were twins. A child had a small bruise on her leg, and the shoemaker asked what had happened to her daughter's leg. She replied that they were not my children but my neighbors. Their parents died in their infancy, and I am raising them. They are like children to me, she added. Then the young man looked at the children carefully and smiled. The young man measured the children's feet, and the children and the woman returned.

The next day the young man came and told the shoemaker, God has forgiven me; I'm going back. The shoemaker said to the young man. I know that you don't look like an ordinary man; I am not authorized to stop you here and on your journey, but please answer me a question.

You've laughed three times since you came here.

You looked at my wife and laughed as the food was served
Second time you laughed when the rich man came
You laughed a third time when that woman and children came
Why did you laugh?
The man replied, what you said is right; I am not an ordinary man.
I am an angel.

One day God told me to bring the spirit of a woman; when I arrived at the woman's house, the view was pathetic. It was not long before she gave birth to two girls who were twins. When she saw me, she realized that it was the angel who had come to take her life. She cried and told me not to take her life now and that my husband had died two days earlier. She screamed again, saying that if I too died, these children would have no one else to look after them. I went back to see the woman crying.

God rebuked me for not taking the woman's life.

God told me to go back and take that woman's life,

Then God said one more thing; you must understand why people live and live on earth for a while.

I went to earth and took that woman's life; her spirit went up out of my hand as I went back with her life.

I was falling in front of this chapel as if someone had pushed me away.

You took me to your house; your wife initially argued but kindly gave me food.

"God was teaching me that kindness is one of the reasons people live."

It was at that realization that I smiled, looking at your wife.

Then I laughed when the rich man came, and when the rich man looked at you and laughed, I saw behind him the angel of death who had come to take his life. Because I knew the rich man would die, he would no longer require a shoe, and I made a sandal for him to wear for his death.

"But I still realized they did not know what they wanted and were fussing over things they did not need."

The third time I laughed when I saw those girls, I took the life of their mother. Although they died, their children were raised by a woman in a nearby house. She had compassion and love for these children. Therefore they did not die.

"God taught that the world does not end when one dies and that they will live as long as there is love in this world; love is what makes human life possible on earth."

Having said this, the young man took the form of an angel and flew to heaven.

Yes, the African diaspora, now the first thing you need to do is show compassion to the country of Africa and **be kind to the African people,** who are from your DNA. Some of your brothers and sisters are struggling for food and clothing, and your small donations can be a treasure. But you should not donate through big organizations because not even 10% of those donations reach their hands. Today the big organization is controlled not by good people but by mafia groups that exploit the African people. These people show the poor face of Africa and collect the bulk of it for the benefit of the mafia; otherwise, where are the billions collected every year? If this money had been used correctly, no hungry people could be found in Africa.

The first step is to drive out the colonialists who are plundering Africa as evil forces. It is important to stand together with one mind through your collective action without thinking of caste, religion, race or politics, or corruption. Africa became independent due to its ancestor's unity in Africa, but do not forget that it is still not wholly free from colonialists. To rebuild Africa, your investments of African descent are essential in every project that Africa needs. The current African governments welcome you to Africa, and the African people love your investment more than anyone else's. This is not the time to blame corruption or some of your incompetent leaders. It would help if you thought about why other countries are investing in Africa despite the problems you think. The greatest weapon of the colonialists is to open the path to fighting each other between castes and religions in each African country. Once they fight each other, they will spend the money on giant advertisements that Africa is not a safe place and that they can loot their asset from there. That is the news you are watching through some of the media.

A great example of this is the destruction of the economy of Zimbabwe by expulsing Muslims and Christians from Zimbabwe and the declaration of the United Nations/US sanctions. Now that Mozambique started exploring the GAS, some groups are also trying to spoil that country. Whose plan is this? The African people as a whole must respond to this. African Americans can play a significant role. If you don't unite and respond now, each African country will face the same problems as Zimbabwe, Mozambique, South Sudan, etc. Do not forget that France and the United Kingdom are the VETO power under United Nations, the former colonialists in Africa. So as an African diaspora, your incredible support will contribute to boosting Africa.

"It is not uncommon for a man to fall into delusion without realizing it."

It is the responsibility of the present good leaders/Presidents of the other African countries to first give the proper guidance to the Zimbabwean hygiene government. If you are not speaking out together as a continent for Zimbabwe today, I would like to remind you of what **Haile Selassie - "Former Emperor of Ethiopia,"** had told when Italians occupied Addis Ababa. **"IF WE TODAY AND YOU TOMORROW"**

About the corruption: The corrupted leaders did not realize that **the angel of death had come to take his life at any time,** without knowing that they were doing their looting job. They believe they will make more than enough for him and his family need can earn through corruption. They do not realize that money should share the poor people's basic needs. The words of the Bible say: "The rich will be filled with riches" those words may be about the leaders like this. They can only make money; they cannot enjoy it, or it is not destined to be passed on to their children or their generation. As soon as it is handed over, that generation will not live long, become addicted to drugs, and suffer misery for themselves.

The corrupted leader will never be happy enough until the legal authority catches them or somebody kills them. They don't know why they make money and how much they want; they will continue their journey. At last, they will not take from this world not more than a white cloth or a suit with a wooden box for the final destination like the same poor people.

Or the previous bad African leaders deposited all their looted money in American and European banks. All of them loosed their invested amount. The Financial crisis of 2007–2008 led to many bank failures in the United States. The Federal Deposit Insurance Corporation (FDIC) closed 465 failed banks from 2008 to 2012. In Europe in 2008, 31 banks were bailed out, and in 2009 a further 13 banks were bailed out. They planned to close the banks because they knew nobody could claim that deposited money. Another billion dollars will be in Swiss banks and the British Virgin Islands that could be for dead leaders or leaders alive today. Even their widows of children cannot claim that money legally. But each country's African government can claim to bring it back.

"Don't wish to get anything for free; it will never stay with you; it is not the fault of the giver to give in vain, but he who gets in vain will be lazy."

Billions of African money loosed because of these evil leaders. They cannot claim it officially because this is not their money; the looted cash may be deposited in some other people's name.

So, you do not have to worry about it; you do your part per God's prescription.

In the minds of ordinary Africans struggling with life in Africa today, there is nothing but love. They have forgotten even the ability to react to the oppression of the colonialists, the only good people living in Africa today who live in mutual love. The power of the ancient Africans would have obeyed even a lion at a glance. The power of those ancestors is hidden somewhere within you.

"It's better to light a candle than curse the darkness"- Chinese Proverb.

The real corruption is done not only to some African leaders but also to former colonialist France. France still doesn't want to leave Africa alone. Why is France controlling ECOWAS countries? All these countries are officially independent; they no longer require France's control; why, because they speak French, does it mean they are France's children? If yes, let France give the same right that the French citizen receives from France to the ECOWAS people.

These ECOWAS country people don't know how to control their country? They don't know read and write or to speak in front of other countries? They are no more babies... so it is better to leave them alone and pay back their money deposited to French Central Bank since their Independence. Once they get their own money from France, ECOWAS will be the wealthiest country in the African Continent; it is the time to claim. Is it not corruption? This is not against humanity?

Now the French government is trying to implement the currency of ECOWAS, replacing it with the French Franc. This decision must make by the African Union, not France. France's duty was over after the independence only task balance was to pay their deposited fund to distribute.

The French Franc was the currency of France from 1795 until 2002 when the Euro replaced it. ... French Francs are now obsolete. From 2002 until today, French Franc is not valid in France even though they are printing for ECOWAS countries and controlling why? Why are United Nations, African Union, or other world leaders not questioning this? Because France is the nuclear power country? Or are they the VETO power member in the United Nations? This was what was mentioned earlier the United Nations Organizations are not doing justice to African Countries.

The 15 members of the Economic Community of West African States (ECOWAS) are Benin, Burkina Faso, Cabo Verde, Cote d'Ivoire,

The Gambia, Ghana, and Guinea, Guinea-Bissau, Liberia, Mali, Niger, Nigeria, Senegal, Sierra Leone, and Togo.

The West African CFA franc is the currency of eight independent states in West Africa: Benin, Burkina Faso, Guinea-Bissau, Ivory Coast, Mali, Niger, Senegal, and Togo. Now France is trying to change it to ECOWAS currency. This is unfair; let African Union or the ECOWAS country leaders take the decision, not France. At least America should disagree with this French interference again African Countries if America believes in United Nations Organizations.

Wake up, African diaspora. It's not too late; this is the time you must take out that power.

THIS TIME FOR AFRICA.........
WAKA WAKA AFRICA......

"Waka Waka" is a phrase used in several parts of Africa and translates most regularly as "Just do it!"

All Africans must listen to this song at least twice in their prayer to get the energy to develop Africa.

https://www.lyrics.com/lyric/20987669/Shakira/Waka+Waka+%28This+Time+For+Africa%29+%5BEnglish+Version

You're a good soldier.
Choosing your battles
Pick <u>yourself</u> up and dust <u>yourself</u> off, and get back in the saddle
You're on the <u>front</u> line
Everyone's watching
You know, serious, we're <u>getting</u> closer; this isn't over.

Today's your day
I feel it
You paved the way
Believe it

"Human behaviors flow from three main sources."
Desire, Emotions, Knowledge. By Plato.

Forget all about the past; there is no point in worrying about it and learning only suitable lessons from it. There is no need to worry about the future if you live by doing the present.

It is time to identify and kick out the colonialists who are making them fight each country and its people in Africa. The very existence of a nation is the unity of the people of that country, and a good leader must make the people unite. It is this commitment that determines the progress of a nation. There may be different opinions between the people and the leaders within the country, and it should be settled between the people and the leaders of that country. The colonialists are taking advantage of this opportunity, do not allow them again.

"Excellence is not a gift, but a skill that takes practice. We do not act rightly because of excellence. We achieve excellence by acting rightly" By Plato.

It is challenging to defeat a country that stands together. This is what our freedom fighters, our forefather Kwame Nkrumah the first President of Ghana, have repeatedly said – **One continent, One Nation, One Army, One Central Bank, One National Anthem, and one Passport for "The United States of Africa"** that is the dream of the forefathers and many of the present leader's vision. Without that, keeping our mother of Africa safe isn't easy. The motto of the colonialists is to divide and rule so that by dividing, they can do everything very quickly. Enslaved people have ruled Africa for centuries, yet some ugly leaders remain in Africa as their shoe lickers; finding them first and removing them will be better; they are the curse for Africa. If the dream of the United States of Africa comes true, then Africa will be the AID supplier to the rest of the world because no other continent has this much wealth.

COVID19 Pandemic made upside most of the countries in the world. Still, to Africa, it looks like a blessing because now all the present African leaders realize that Africa is more significant than any other country in terms of health by nature with the immune power (be proud that you have black skin, one of the reason COVID19 not effected many of the African people because of the black skin with better immune power, maybe China made this virus especially to attack the white people – Former US President Donald Trump also called as COVID-19) and slowly opened their eyes and looking down to the earth of Africa. All these years, most leaders thought that without Europe, America, or Asia, they could not do anything in Africa. They went after others without knowing the value of the food on their plate for so long. Just for a few months, some African leaders could not meet, or the colonial leaders could not meet African leaders; within this period, African leaders realized that they were better than others– Thanks to COVID19 and its upcoming variant yet to come.

The Global Race in Africa

The real-world global power knows the next potential growth continent with 17% of the world population, 9.6% of global oil output, 90% of world platinum supply, 90% of the world's cobalt supplies, half of the world gold suppliers, two-thirds of the world's manganese, 35% of the world's uranium supplies, 75% of world Colton supplies and 54 votes in the united nations general assembly is what Africa attractive yet Africa still poor in front of the world and the citizen of Africa still hunger and poverty.

The new teams have already arrived in Africa, Israel, Canada, and Japan on top of France, the United States, China, Belgium, and India. Among all one country that is China is colonizing one-third of the African continent with its unity power and money to become the winner of the 21st century. China is funding infrastructure projects one in every third project. China had already invested over 2 trillion US dollars in African building railways. China sells Chinese currencies to over 33 countries and teaches mandarin with 54 Confucius centers in Africa. At least ten thousand firms operate in Africa. Over ten thousand Chinese troops were already based in Africa to protect the Chinese people. China is not the only investor in Africa; the United States is one of the most prominent investors in Africa, with over

54 billion US Dollars in FDI stocks. Over 600 American companies operating in South Africa Alone and over 7000 trouped deployed in the African continent. How Many African diaspora companies and investments are in African Continent? India opened 18 new embassies in the African continent; India was the only country that supported the African anti-colonial struggle to get Freedom from the colonialists with the support of Mahatma Gandhi soon after the Indian independence. India is offering 50000 scholarships in New Delhi for African students.

People may ask this question again; despite all these superpowers being there in these small countries in Africa but why are these superpowers not able to find and control the terrorist groups? Are these small number of terrorist groups much more substantial than all these superpowers?????

Everyone wants Africa's wealth, but nobody wants African people other than for their slavery jobs. Where is the African diaspora?????? Now all the weapons sellers realized that African leaders could pay the money from Africa because they had already spoiled the Middle East, and not much income was expected from the Middle East, only from the Oil resources, and Africa has everything.

In the past, enslaved people were taken from Africa to many countries to be enslaved. Still, after the end of slavery, all superpowers became changed their plan to make the African people be enslaved people within Africa itself.

Warning to the African Leaders and its people.

Things that all leaders need to understand in the future: To succeed, you must distinguish between prey and predator. The community includes victims and hunters. The same person may have come in the form of a game and hunter. In life, we are often not victims but failures. Many succeed by preying on the hunter's tricks; once the victim fails without learning from them, the thief and the police do not understand the game. We often do not even realize that we are being victimized. The question for many is, how do we recognize a hunter's trick? How can we escape from it?

We see such hunters all the time, and hunters are waiting for us with prey that we do not even realize are preying on us. Some are waiting to conquer us physically, socially, financially, and mentally. Many fail, not because they lack ideas or skills, but because they understand the hunter's intrigues and do not respond promptly. Not only must we not die, but we must also be able to maintain what we have achieved.

Africa is a deep well that never runs dry, so now is not the time to mourn our losses. We will not get back anything that we lost but keep losing nothing again. Now is the time to make decisions for the country's good, as if on a war footing. Now that you have identified those holding you back for centuries, you must make every move with them with skepticism and careful decision-making.

"These are the most influential presidents of the 21ˢᵗ century to Africa that the people of Africa must be proud of: These three presidents can bring/brought up Africa to develop Africa into a prosperous continent.

- **Paul Kagame – President of Rwanda**
- **Nana Akufo-Addo – President of Ghana**
- **John Pombe Magufuli(Late)**

Many wars worldwide are caused by words that are sharper than weapons. All the leaders and the people of that country can live in peace with their neighbors if they pay special attention to this. The enemy selects spies from that same country to disrupt such peace. It is a wise solution for each Government to appoint specially selected spies from that country to identify such spies. Because of such spies, every country has perished and is still dying. Eliminating these spies is the first duty of good leaders in every country because God dwells in a clean place.

Africa Agenda 2063

The African Union is made up of 55 Member States, which represent all the countries on the African continent. The declaration marked the re-dedication of Africa towards the attainment of the Pan African Vision of an integrated, prosperous, and peaceful Africa, driven by its citizens, representing a dynamic force in the international arena, and Agenda 2063 is the concrete manifestation of how the continent intends to achieve ... GOD SAVE AFRICA.

To know more about the Goals & Priority Areas of Agenda 2063 Visit the African Union Website: https://au.int/en/agenda2063/goals.

The African Union's vision is: "An integrated, prosperous and peaceful Africa, driven by its citizens and representing a dynamic force in the global arena." Africa's challenges include improving education, healthcare, HIV/AIDs, agriculture, building science and technology centers, providing adequate housing, conflict resolution - peace and stability, and so forth.

"Ask not what your country can do for you – ask what you can do for your country,"- said John F. Kennedy.

The good of a country does not depend only on the ability of its President or the government officials alone, but on the people of that country's togetherness, support, and unity. The African Union has been effective in boosting cooperation and unity within Africa, putting its efforts towards diminishing conflict and promoting democracy. ... Processes are also being implemented that aim to reduce corruption and increase credibility amongst African leaders.

"A gemstone takes on its appearance with thousands of cuts on the outside and shines beautifully when the unwanted is cut off. If a few leaders belong to this gem or want to be like a gem, you will have to cut out many flaws and habits; of course, it can sometimes be excruciating, but it's necessary for the betterment of Africa."

Be a part of this 2063 Mission.

"The citizens of Africa or the African diaspora must not ask the leaders in Africa what you are going to do for me; rather, it is the moral responsibility of each African citizen to ask themselves what I can do for Africa," which reminds the word of Martin Luther King.

Waka Waka Africa......Just Do It..........

(Waka waka means – do it, in the Central African Language,)

African diaspora.... Your contribution to guidance is very much significant to the African Continent. As mentioned in the previous pages, Millions of African descent spread worldwide. Each people collected 5 US dollars each; earlier, it was impossible, but now you have a platform **https://ouraddi.org/** - The ADDI (The African Diaspora Development Institute) is already going to be Billions of Dollars. It is better to associate with the African Union and propose the investment plan and your demands, which can improve Africa and benefit the African diaspora worldwide. There are many ways for an investment plan. For example, it can be a model of shares and bonds starting from even 5 dollars. So, the people can purchase the shares per their capacity from 100 to 10000 or more.

Let the AID send out from African mothers to the World...

All these years European Union or some other countries claims that Africa is poor, so they are feeding Africa and its people. But the truth is Africa is providing not only most of the European countries but to America and Asia with the mineral assets for their manufacturing. Most of the minerals are exploited through the colonial agenda by making millions from the used assets and distributing little AID to hide their exploitation. If these exploiting areas are protected, then Africa can send millions of AID every year from Africa to the rest of the poor people around the world.

There is no virtue other than imparting knowledge:

The diasporas can take the responsibility to educate the children of Africa, starting with schools, Colleges, Industrial Training Institutes, Information Technology Centers, and Engineering Colleges. The advantage is that even for the educated young diaspora, after graduation, you are looking for a job in the place where you are now may be hard to get the job. Those teams can make the associations, come to Africa, and teach your brothers and sisters. That can be your job as well as the charity for Africa. Remember 55 Countries in African Continent, each country thinks of 100 educational institutions, which means 5500 institutions with the support of the African Union and African Development Bank. So, you have already created the job for at least 55000 teachers or professors and other employees, another 55000 directly and indirectly, the school buses, accommodations, vehicle maintenance workshops, etc.

Health Care Sector: Most leaders and rich African people depend on Europe, America, or Asia for treatment. Don't you think it is a vast opportunity to build Medical Colleges and therapy with your investments? Off-Course each African Government and the African Union will love this opportunity. There are not enough doctors in Africa. There are no investors from the African diaspora in Africa. At least ten multi-specialty Hospitals in each country mean 550 Hospitals. Don't you think this is a massive opportunity with your investments? How much millions of money spending on health care systems from Africa, but other continents do not enjoy all these benefits? Countries, especially the Chinese, presently occupy these opportunities. Why can't you take this opportunity? Five hundred fifty multi-Specialty hospitals can create another 100,000 jobs at least. Moreover, Africa's health care system will improve. Then you don't need an AID from United Nations, Europe, or America.

You don't have to be worried about when you get free Medical AID from other countries or their mercy. The history shows testing of any drugs: - First testing with Rat, cat or dogs, monkeys then the medical companies immediately coming to test with Africans without your knowledge.

- Why are African people are their testing lab?
- Why did all these viruses' AIDS, Ebola, Sears, etc........ find Africa first?
- First, they make the medicine, then release the virus, maybe? **God only knows.....**

"COVID19 is the only virus that came out before the vaccination, which is why it is not found first in Africa".

It can be true or may not be true.........you can think of it as just an assumption...

So, when Africa has its research centers, Africa can produce the medicine and vaccinations with Africa itself.

"You are what you eat" if that is true, Africans eat different food, and Europeans and Americans or Asians eat other food. Then how the European or American-made medicine will be suitable for the African body? Why not African treatment not ideal for Africans?

It has been noted recently that when Madagascar found the herbal medicine for COVID19, the international Medical Commission or World Health Organization would not want to approve it and make lousy propaganda against Madagascar. But fortunately, Madagascar, Tanzania, Sudan, and most African countries are free from Covid19 before any other countries, and they started their routine. However, still, many American, European, and Asian Countries are struggling with COVID-19. It is proven that Herbal and Ayurveda medicine will never make any side effects even if it is not cured. It can also be true or not, you can think... Why is the United Nations Health Organization not paying attention to African inventions?

Africa must need to Unite:

After the independence, America became united and Made the United States of America. India became the Republic of India, China became the Republic of China, and Europe became Schengen Countries/European Union. Many other countries became one, but only Africa was still nowhere, even though there is a big organization called AU- African Union. Unfortunately, the actions of the African Union's activities are not presentable enough to the continent, African people, and the world. Or the colonialist agenda not to unite Africa together? After the African independence of most of the African countries, many leaders tried to build Africa. **Over 28 Presidents were killed or removed from power after the Independence**

of most of the African Countries. Whoever raises the voice to build Africa, all of them are no more or settled in the USA or Europe, becoming the silent cat.

The reason was that no one was there to support these leaders or bring this case to the international court, so the agenda of the colonialists was still on the road. Whose fault is it? African diaspora's..... You are the main responsible. Once you get a better living, you have forgotten the past and your DNA struggling in Africa.

"People without the knowledge of their History, Origin, and Culture is like a tree without roots" By Marcus Garvey.

You must understand that the people in Africa are incapable of doing big things or such significant developments because they are still underfoot by the colonialists looking for the bread crunch to fill their bellies. Nobody is there to support or help them from the diaspora's end. Therefore, they are still poor. Once you give a hand to them, they will be ready to sacrifice their entire life with you. That is so generous the African people are.

Let me share the unity of the people of the smallest state in India, Kerala: Over 30% of the Keralite people are working worldwide. Over 96% of the people can read and write that 70% of Kerala's development investments come from these Diasporas. Kerala's population is Over 35 million people. Over 5 million people are working out of Kerala. There have been 111 climate-related natural disasters that have recently caused at least $1 billion in damage. In all these disasters, the significant contribution came from the Kerala diaspora supported regardless of Religion, Cast, or ethnicity. Kerala Diasporas are willing to help Kerala by tightening their belts over their bellies. That shows their commitment to their birthplace.

Regardless of any ruling parties controlling the Kerala State Government, the Government school children are getting free Education, Free food up to the 12th grade, and Free Medicine within their capacity. **By the way, some Indian states are even poorer than Africa because of some bad political leaders.** African diaspora must adopt this idea of the Kerala system to implement in Africa.

- You may be hearing, or maybe it is true, that African children are not getting a good education and good food?
- Just think about what you have done for them until now?
- Have you ever felt shame when BBC, CNN, or other international channels showed that Africa is poor?
- When your brothers and sisters become hungry, how can you eat without sharing them?

It may not be your fault; it was the responsibility of your parents to share the stories of the history of Africa. Never mind, you still have time to do something for Africa.

It is noted that the recent aggression against Chinese Investors in some of the African Countries. This is the real bad politics of the western world and Americans. The African people must realize that because of the Chinese people, some of the countries have become colorful, and few African people's hungers has changed a little. Because of their strategic investments, good roads, railways, stadiums, etc., are coming up. It is not the Chinese investor's fault they are making more profit. Investors are always looking for profit. As an African diaspora, what kind of investment was done in Africa when Africa was bleeding. Few Asian countries had invested, but the Europeans and Americans were looting the minerals, including Oil and Gas, from all over Africa. Now the formal colonialists started their plan to make the fight against the Chinese and Africans together so that countries' economies would spoil. That country will go into disaster, and they can continue lootings the assets again and another opportunity to sell their weapons in Africa. This is happening in Iraq, Iran, Syria, Lebanon, Libya, Yemen, South Sudan, the Republic of Congo, etc. you can see no buildings, hospitals, schools, or homes left there, and people become refugees and waiting for the mercy of the United Nations and the charitable organizations. African leaders or the diaspora must not allow this colonial agenda to implement anymore in Africa.

You must understand that the problem makers in Africa are not the Chinese or other Asian people; it is only the Western colonialist agenda. Because the Chinese were investing, but European's job was only looting the assets; because of Chinese involvement in many African

Countries, European were unable to reach the same as the Chinese, so the Colonialist spread bad propaganda or spent money on advertisements or some internal bad political people to spoil the Chinese business. Of course, like any others, all the Chinese investors are not 100% clear in terms of business. It is the responsibility of the real leaders in each country to control them to protect the country's interests and people's rights, as President Paul Kagame of Rwanda did. He had deported some of the Chinese people from Rwanda because they had shown the same colonialist mentality to the Rwandan people of formal slavery. Wrong is always not acceptable to any people regardless of nationality; everyone must respect and obey each country's rules.

Chinese are the business-minded people, not the colonialists, but through their business, they are colonizing Africa and filling their people. Some of the Study says at the time of 2050, the Chinese population will go high, and it will be challenging to accommodate all the Chinese within China. So, they are looking for another country to live in. The formal colonialist plan was to remove Chinese business people who were investing heavily and getting contracts, which the Europeans could not compete with the Chinese by all means. Colonial people knew if Africa developed by any means, it would be a tragedy for Europe. So, they are trying their best to spoil Africa's development. Do not fall on the agenda of the colonialists; Colonialists are always like the deadly virus to Africa; it is your responsibility to find the vaccination to prevent that virus first, then only Africa gets cured. It is better to keep China as the vaccination to avoid European colonialists as another strong Virus.

"By all means, both the virus is dangerous to Africa, but it is your intelligence to control both the virus to make the antibiotics to cure Africa."

Over 60 years, Europe had never done anything other than loot the assets, divide, and kill African descent. If they had done something, those are all for their better living and benefits only, not for the betterment of African people, and they had not done anything free, or they brought their investments from their own country. All are looted from the same African countries themselves. You can control Chinese people within your capacity, but you will not be able to handle these European colonial parasites.

Africa needs financial support for sure, be with the investors who are flexible and get befitted for Africa. But make sure you are not surrendering Africa again to any other country for a few of your temporary benefits. All kinds of loans are always a liability, even with the short interest; before taking the loan, the borrower must make to find the opportunity to pay back, not the collateral guarantee will go to the investor, which is common in the investment and banking sector. China is brilliant in this field with their corked-minded ideas in the field of investments with their money. Some of the countries are already in the investment trap of China.

Here we go......

Sri Lanka: Loans from China to build the Hambantota Port in Sri Lanka has been cited as an example of debt-trap diplomacy after Sri Lanka defaulted and subsequently gave a 99-year lease to China in place of payment. Sri Lanka is often portrayed as a country that fell into a debt trap due to public investment projects financed by China. ... Sure enough, Hambantota port was not making enough revenue to repay China when loan payments came due.

Zambia: Trade between China and Zambia increased in 2010 to US$2.2 billion. Chinese investments in Zambia range from mining interests in Zambia's copper belt to agriculture, manufacturing, and tourism investments. As of February 2011, 25 farms in Zambia are being run by Chinese entities. Zambia had accumulated loans from China totaling almost 6.4 billion USD in end-2017. If this figure is correct, Zambia may have a total debt of 14.7 billion (including state-guaranteed loans), of which Chinese loans account for some 44%. Most notably, Chinese firms are seeking to capitalize on the liquidation of Konkola Copper Mines, a subsidiary of London-based Vedanta Resources.

Zimbabwe's debt is $7 billion, or over 200% of the country's GDP. However, this figure is disputed, with figures as high as $11 billion being quoted once debts to other African countries and China are included.

Ghana receives ¢ 22.2bn Chinese support. Ghana has received an interest-free loan of 20 million yuan RMB (¢ 22.195 billion) from the Chinese government.

The World Bank recently released data on official debt to China in 37 African countries. By the first quarter of 2009, China had canceled 150 such loans owed by 32 African countries. In 2018, Chinese President Xi Jinping announced forgiveness of all intergovernmental zero-interest loans for least-developed African countries with diplomatic relations with China.

Solution for Investments

Chinese or any other countries loan can be welcomed to Africa, but this is not the right permanent solution to protect Africa; it can be a strategic partnership of 50-50% for 15 to 20 years of profit-sharing for any project basis, after that the same project must be entirely handed over to the same government and its people. Africa has a lot of wealth, and no money to invest is fine; let the investors share the benefit 50% as their investment benefit for a certain period only and 100% ownership with the same government. After that, the investor must hand over the project peacefully to the concerned government will is a wise idea. This is one example; there are high-ranked African people within the country and abroad and Diasporas working around the world as bankers and economists and put their suggestions to Africa for her developments. Or the governments must take the advice from successful advisors like DR. PLO Lumumba, Rutendo Benson Matinyarere, Dr. Arikna Chihombori Quao, and many more. The reason is that the advisors know about Africa's pulse, and that advice can get from the people who studied very well about Africa and her people. The Vision Africa 2063 is the best move ever made in African history, but getting support from the diaspora worldwide is essential.

All African diaspora must consider what contribution can be given to protect Africa, or else China or any other colonizers will legally colonize Africa. These debts are not huge compared to the assets available in Africa. Just one or two years of exploration and Mining of Minerals are sufficient to clear all the obligations to pay back and protect Africa. Because it is a known fact that some of the European countries still loot the assets and the hard cash from Africa every year, over 500 billion dollars, the present whole African continent debt may be less than that. So, strategic planning is essential; the advisory board must be of African descent only recommended.

Do you ever note the group of street dogs and lions when they see the food? It is a different approach.

When they see the food, even though there is enough food to eat for them, the dogs fight each other while eating, no matter what the others are their cablings, and also, they don't care if it is fresh or not. But even if the dog has good quality, he will be grateful and loyal to his master. Some political leaders have the same attitude when they see the money and are dedicated to the colonialists by surrendering their brothers and sisters and the country itself.

But the lion never fights each other for food, they always hunt and wait for the leader of their family to come to share with their group, and they care about others by leaving the rest. There are outstanding political leaders in Africa like that, lions.

Leadership quality in Lion,

- The number one factor is confidence and belief; while he runs behind an animal,
- He never believes that he will fail.
- He is ready to take the challenges and risks until he achieves it
- He is not afraid of his life at that moment
- He typically hunts more giant animals than him
- He never eats the fermented food
- He is not only hunting for himself but also dependent on the other.
- He will protect his dependence and the boundaries
- Finally, once his belly is complete, he will never hunt unnecessarily until he becomes hungry.

This is why the Lion becomes the king or the leader in the forest.

"Africa still missing the Lions attitude leaders at this century" Even though they belong to a generation of ancestors that even trembled at the lion.

For that, the mother of Africa called all the diaspora to unite to make One Continent, One Nation, One Army, One Heart, and One soul. That is **THE UNITED STATES OF AFRICA.**

DEVELOPMENT IN AFRICA

For a country to be economically developed, investment from that country or abroad is essential. If buying from other countries is to come to that country, that country must be peaceful. The colonialists aim to destroy peace here or to proclaim that this country is not safe. For centuries they would have used this propaganda as their weapon of war, and they had succeeded in it, and it continues to this day in some African countries.

"The colonialists roamed all over Africa like horses that no one could tame, but their prowess was lessened by the arrival of some warrior leaders who could tame even the wild lion with a single stick or a glance."

It should not be forgotten that despite this unrest and political anarchy, some countries are willing to invest in Africa, including China, India, and some Arab countries. Their goal was, of course, to make a profit from their investment. They know that such profits can only be made from such countries by risking their assets so that they can make huge profits as soon as possible. The only benefit to Africa from this is that it has to a certain extent, helped alleviate the hunger of several poor people, and some bad political leaders made millions of shares from this gambling game. In the meantime, Chinese colonies and investment can still be seen in many African countries.

"But the fact is that the leaders of those African countries have not been able to make the benefit to Africa and her people." Only a ruler who controls the five senses can protect the country and the people. Gentleness and humility are needed for sensual success.

It is not to these investors to show their current hatred or animosity and will not contribute to the country's growth. Instead, it's wise to change the rules to benefit Africa and its people so that more nations will invest in Africa and have more jobs for young people. The truth is that until recently, the African diaspora did not remember Africa or its growth, nor did many leaders try to convey Africa's sorrows. This may be due to the lack of good leaders.

Africa - the Sleeping Giant slowly waking up

Now things are changing in Africa because of some great visionary leaders properly implementing their plan; as a result, the following countries are coming up and removing poverty from Africa. Some African countries economies have been growing from 6% to 8% yearly for a few years.

Few of the performing countries in the African Continent.

- South Sudan
- Rwanda
- Côte d'Ivoire
- Ethiopia
- Senegal
- Benin
- Uganda
- Kenya
- Mozambique
- Burkina Faso

Every time Africa tried to rise, the colonialists tried to pit that country against each other. Meanwhile, we have all seen a reflection in recent times. It has led to conflicts with South Sudan, Ethiopia,

Uganda, and Rwanda are live examples of this 21st century. But the leaders are smart enough to control at the beginning because they know this problem initiating from where and they have seen it many times.

"Often, long-term decisions by good leaders are for the good of the nation and the people of that country. Those who disagree with it may call that leader evil and wicked, and many exceptions may be heard, and sometimes they have to go through all that and make decisions".

Some great leaders' long vision in Africa will remove the poverty of Africa and build the image in front of the world. Other countries see only the pictures through the media that Africa is poor. But some of the press, including African channels, do not want to project the development through the great leader's tremendous contributions even though the colonialists and the wrong political leaders within the countries are trying to spoil the economy. But this leader takes this attitude, **"The dogs are barking, and the camel is walking"** they know the journey cannot stop because of hearing the dog's voice barking.

"The wise man should not be afraid of anyone; no matter how powerful he is, he can face it wisely."

Paul Kagame: KIGALI, Rwanda — Twenty-five years after the start of its genocide, in which some 800,000 people were killed, Rwanda is rebuilding with hope and shines in a new light, said President Paul Kagame. Speaking at commemoration services. Kagame said that **"Rwandans would never turn against each other again."**

This is known as leadership; Rwanda's parliament has the highest percentage of women in a single house parliament worldwide. The government has reserved 24 out of the 80 seats in the Chamber of Deputies for women. Since 2003 Rwanda's Constitution has required women to hold 30 percent of elected positions. Today, with 49 women in parliament, that figure is 61 percent—the highest in the world. Four of the seven Supreme Court seats are held by women. The government also has promoted gender equality in Rwanda using the Ministry of Gender and Family Promotion. In one significant change, women have been given the same right as men to inherit the land and in other factors like in some government posts, the military, and education.

John Pombe Magufuli took charge as the fifth President of Tanzania.

The slogan for this President – was "Africa is not poor" During the SADC (Southern African Development Community) submission, he reminded all the African Presidents and leaders that the natural resources in Africa are enormous. But none of the African countries are industrializing this mineral. Instead, all the countries are exporting it. He mentioned that natural resources export means we are exporting jobs. This is why Africa is poor, and the young generation is struggling with employment and depending on other countries for survival. The 2015 to 2063 SADC submitted decided to Industrialize Africa to be independent. The Visionary leader expressed the interest in supporting the surplus food products from Tanzania to other African Countries to reduce the import from different regions and advised that all the countries be independent in food production to remove poverty.

President John Pombe Magufuli, A great example of being a man of the country is his reduced salary from $15000 to 4000 dollars. He is against corruption; Tanzania's anti-corruption watchdog suspended nine senior staff, including architects, construction managers, and quantity surveyors, over claims of corruption related to the construction of the agency's seven district buildings. But this brave warrior said goodbye to this earth, donating only a few good things and serving from 2015 until his death in July 2021.

African Free Trade:

The African Continental Free Trade Area (ACFTA) in the Kigali-Rwanda conference in March 2018 came into effect. 52 out of 55 countries have signed the agreement, and 18 have ratified it. Twenty-two countries must approve the deal for it to go into effect. The world's largest free trade area, encompassing 54 countries and 1.2 billion people, the African Continental Free Trade Area will bring the promise of trade-led economic growth closer to reality for Africa's entrepreneurs, industrialists, investors, innovators, and service suppliers.

African diaspora...Wake up and smell the coffee.
"It is easier to move the ship when the favorable wind."

Yes, this is a good time to invest in Africa with the support of the present visionary leaders who are sacrificing their lives to bring up Africa and her people for those glorious days. As a diaspora, it is part of your responsibility to support these present leaders.

"Remember that your contribution is more valuable to your leaders than investors in any other country."

What better country could you be safer than investing in your home country of Africa?

Remember that on other continents such as Europe, America, Asia, etc., manufacturing companies are producing many products using raw materials from Africa. Such countries would not even exist without Africa. Without Africa, at least 50% of the production will not come out. So as the African diaspora, do not forget that your investment and, beyond that, your experience are essential for the rise of Africa. Your investment, your education, your inventions, and your intelligence will all benefit Africa. This is it, do not miss this opportunity to prove your skills in front of other countries.

African Diaspora (DNA) around the world.

- Peru: 1.2 Million
- Mexico 1.3 Million
- United Kingdom: 2 Million
- Jamaica: 2.7 Million
- Venezuela: 3.4 Million
- France: 5 Million
- Colombia: 5.3 Million
- Haiti: 11 Million
- United States of America: 46.3 Million
- Brazil: 83.2 Million

Some of the great leaders sacrificed their lives for freedom for you,

Black leaders like Nelson Mandela sacrificed his life of 27 years in Jail fighting for Freedom for the black people, and he achieved it.

Martin Luther King sacrificed his life for the Black people's freedom. Same like that some of these leaders of the African continent: KWAME NKRUMAH OF GHANA, Haile Selassie - Former Emperor of Ethiopia, JULIUS KAMBARAGE NYERERE OF TANZANIA, JOMO KENYATTA – Father of Kenya, ROBERT MUGABE OF ZIMBABWE (FORMER – Sothern Rhodesia), "THOMAS SANKARA" of Burkina Faso, Kenneth David Buchizya Kaunda of Zambia, Samuel Shafishuna Daniel Nujoma of Namibia, José Eduardo dos Santos of Angola, Samora Moisés Machel of Mozambique and many more also sacrificed their lives to get the freedom from the colonialist.

Almost all the African countries are awaiting your arrival; if you want to see what real love means, you must meet African Fathers and mothers and your brothers and sisters in Africa. You have only seen this kind of love in your dreams or movies, and you have to go there and experience it.

Remember, don't think you are going for a job in Africa as a first step. That may not be so easy at the moment. This is the time to go to any African country as an investor. A little money can do a perfect business compared to America or any other European country.

Opportunities will never come; know your door always; it comes only a few times. This is the time; it may be too late if you don't go now. Because Chinese, Indian, European, and Japanese are already there, they are just waiting to open the borders to implement the African Free Trade Area to start their branches in 54 countries with their investments. The only missing people are the children of the African diaspora. The soles of the forefathers and mother of Africa need you more than anyone in Africa. That's what your forefather's vision is to be one United Africa without borders, one unity, one Army, one Military with one powerful Africa nobody can beat in terms of workforce and wealth.

Remember: **"God will never close one door before opening the other two doors; people don't see the open doors because they cry behind the closed door asking why you closed my door"** So take it positively. You must welcome the present racial problems in America and some other countries to open your eyes to America because you believe that your other two doors are already open. Only you have to find out where those doors are.

Let me remind you of a story:

A frog was living in the village water well. One day, a man saw a frog lying in the water and threw it away when he got water from the well. Unexpectedly, the frog came out of the well and tried to jump back into the well in total panic. But due to the height of the well, the frog could not jump back into the well despite its best efforts. The frog was searching for a new home to live in, and he found everything strange in front of him. Some children threw stones at it on the way, but the frog escaped and wandered for two or three days without food.

The frog wandered in search of a lower well and eventually ended up in a large lake. The frog jumped for joy at the sight of the lake and began to swim in the lake. From then on, the frog started to think and thus cursed the old well.

"I have been lying in the small well for so long; here is more than enough food and a spacious atmosphere."

Yes, you feel the same as the frog once you try to settle in Africa. The Choice is yours; of course, it may not be easy to adjust initially, and you may have to make some sacrifices and adjustments in the front, but eventually, you feel the same as the frog.

The best option is to make your city in Africa with the selected African countries with that governmental support. For sure, they will welcome those ideas. That will be your own home and the shopping centers, health clubs, beaches, and whatever you need as per your capacity.

You can copy The Perl Qatar Project to Africa: https://www.visitqatar.qa/discover/tourist-hotspots/the-pearl-qatar.html.

The works started in August 2004 and were complete on the 6th of July 2006. The construction concept opted for the 'Pearl-Qatar' project differs substantially from other artificial island developments in the Middle East. The Pearl-Qatar infrastructure was built to resemble a string of pearls in recognition of the historical pearl-diving sites upon which the island complex is built. Developed by United Development Company, the Island is located 350 meters offshore of Doha's West Bay Lagoon area. In 2004, when the project was first revealed, the initial cost of constructing the island stood at $2.5 billion. Qatar Government is now inviting investors to occupy their homes by spending very little money. The fantastic design and construction will give you that you are living your dream world.

This is the final warning and information for African Diaspora.

The next era belongs to Africa; Africa will be better with or without the African Diaspora. If you come to Africa now, you will get a share of it too, because new mega infrastructure projects construction of Power Projects, Road and Railways, Solar farm power projects, Container terminal ports, Oil refineries, Info Park and Data Centers, New brilliant City constructions, Stadiums, Bridges, etc.; have already been launched in many countries as part of Africa upgrade with the investment over $500 Billion projects. At the end of 2030, you will see the new version of Africa looking better than Europe and Singapore, with many job opportunities. "Mark my word (2020) in your diary and check after eight years."

"You can either be a player or just a spectator, and you can blame others with a little knowledge about Africa."

Because now, most of the major investors are Chinese and Europeans for new megaprojects. African diaspora's presence is not at all there in Africa for the upcoming mega projects.

A businessman in Nigeria-Africa is strong, intelligent, kind, and a long visionary.

Alhaji Aliko Dangote of Nigeria

"Africa is full of opportunities" is one of the precious words from Aliko Dangote.

The wealthiest man in Nigeria and 23rd richest man in the world in the 21st century. Alhaji Aliko Dangote GCON is a Nigerian businessman and philanthropist who is the founder and chairman of Dangote Group, an industrial conglomerate in Africa. Unlike other African people, he did not hide his money and assets in some other countries. He proudly invested his money into the business on his land. Over 25000 job opportunities were created because of his kind generosity and promising to expand the job opportunities to around 180000 in five years. This is what each African people are making money from their source should think and live like a lion, not like a fox. If all the African people believed like Aliko Dangote, with their government's support, Africa would arise like a sphinx bird to support the country's economy, and no one will be hungry anymore.

Nigeria is one of the world's biggest oil exporters, but unfortunately, there is no refinery to feed their domestic consumption of oil products. One of Aliko Dangote's visions is that Nigeria is to be self.

It depended on producing all the products which the country needed. Aliko Dangote had spread his wings into a business in over 16 African countries and bought mining licenses. He invested all his money into the business; yes, cash is not to hide somewhere in the bank; it must also be used for the goodness of the people.

Ongoing projects in Africa:
Nigeria

Aliko Dangote's dream come true in Nigeria

Twelve billion Dollar – Dangote Oil Refinery in Lagos, Nigeria, will process over 650 barrels daily and its related Petrochemical projects for Nigeria's domestic and international use. This will be the biggest oil refinery in Africa and the world's single drain facility. Although Nigeria was the biggest oil producer in Nigeria, there was no oil refinery in Nigeria until 2020. The Dangote Group of Companies owns the investment with the support of the local international bank's loan facility, Standard Chartered Bank, and the United States Trade Development Agency. Dangote Oil Refinery will produce, Gasoline, Diesel, Jet fuel, and its related products. Over 9000 people will get the job opportunity directly and over 25000 jobs indirectly.

Nigeria

5.8 billion Dollar – Mambilla Hydroelectric Power Station Nigeria: This power plant can serve electricity to almost all the areas of Nigeria.

This power station will provide job opportunities to over 50000 people directly and indirectly.

DR Congo

One hundred billion Dollars - Grand Inga Dam III, one of the world's most significant Hydro Mega Electric projects, is one of the largest waterfalls in the world. This will produce approximately 3250 Megawatt per month, which can serve the electric power to many African countries. It means the manufacturing sector will boom in entire Africa.

Pointe Nore Special Economic Zone Congo – This is the 9000 acres of infrastructure development project, including the seaport. This will boost the manufacturing in this country to bring the economy up. This will create over 100,000 jobs for the citizens of Congo.

Egypt

Fifty-eight billion Dollars - Egypt New Capital City, is a new 750 square Kilometers mega new capital city project located 35 kilometers from Cairo City. This smart city includes over 40 small towns within this area, an Airport and Military base, a New Parliament House, Residential and Hotel buildings and apartments, a Mosque, Churches, Stadiums, Over 2000 educational institutions, a Technology and innovation park, Hospitals, and clinics, four-time bigger than the Disney land theme park, 90 square kilometers of Solar Electric Farm, etc. This city in Egypt is going to be the most beautiful in Africa.

Ethiopia

4.8 billion Dollar - Grand Ethiopian DAM- Hydro Electric power project will be one of the largest power plants in Africa and the 7th largest in the world. Upon completion of this project, around 20000 jobs will create from this power plant.

Kenya

Fourteen billion Dollar - Konza Technology City: This is to attract technology partners to invest in Kenya Nairobi. Software development, Data Centers, Disaster recovery centers, etc.

Over 10 billion Dollar - Kenya Standard Gauge Railway will connect Kenya cities and neighboring countries Uganda, South Sudan, Republic of Congo, Rwanda, and Burundi. In the future, it may relate to Addis Ababa, Ethiopia.

Angola

4.5 billion Dollar - Caculo Cabana Hydroelectric Plant — This power plant will produce 2170-megawatt power to serve electric power to the entire country.

These are just a few of the ongoing projects in Africa. This is just the beginning. You should not forget that most investments are from Chinese and European companies. They are investing in Africa, not for the benefit of Africa as a charity; they will ensure they will get a significant chunk out of it. Some countries receive loans from these investors with a long-term contract of 50 to 100 years. It means Africa is moving officially to the same colonizers for her development and lack of investments. If you, the African diaspora willing to invest in your continent will not be surrender to the colonizers again. The investment comes from the investors to make the infrastructure. The profit will generate from that infrastructure, which means they again mind the gain from your own country, which you and your generation are supposed to benefit from and enjoy it.

It is not too late to go and invest in Africa because the manufacturing will start after the infrastructure. The locally manufactured items will be consumed chiefly by African people only. Because the investment is not from your own country, there is a chance of cost increase which African people will struggle with. All this improvement progress happened through some visionary leaders who are currently controlling Africa. And the leaders like Professor PLO Lumumba continuously educate the African people about the progress of Africa.

CHAPTER - 12

AWAKE ARISE AFRICAN DIASPORA

"This is a universal truth; even a 'mother does not love other children as much as she loves her child, if there is, it will be at least a few percent less. If there are mothers whose is not reducing even that few percentages, then she is not only a 'mother' but a saint."

Only African DNA can love Africa, and one thing to remember when someone tells you they love you is because they want some reward from you. So do not get into that trap again.

For many centuries many have loved and killed Africa and her children. Probably because of the increased love, they have enslaved you and transplanted you to too many lands. So many of African descent have forgotten Africa and live in many countries as the diaspora.

They appeared before you in the form of angels with white bodies and black hearts. They taught the African people that all gods are white. So many African leaders forgot their people and became slaves to these white demons. Leaders who were supposed to help the African people forgot themselves and became slaves to the food and luxuries of white devils.

A few generations of enslaved people died; even while living as enslaved people, they had a hope in their minds that they would be set free forever now that freedom had been achieved. The new generation is now living as untouchable and unrecognized in those countries.

Even the animals of the African wilderness are allowed to eat their food, but those white demons are still denied to humans in Africa. Africa's precious metals and forest resources are so much more than that; they plunder even the best people in Africa. White demons who have forgotten humanity for African wealth are still killing the African people. Is it because they are being rewarded that even many high-ranking countries are not reacting against it? There is only air and light on earth for Africans to claim as their own; these are the only two things that whites cannot capture from Africa as a whole.

I Sebastian Joseph – Author of this book. As an Indian, I must tell the truth about what I have seen in Africa and what I am doing currently in Africa.

African Culture is almost like the old culture of Kerala–South India; I am pointing to ancient Kerala because 35 to 40 years before, most Kerala families lived like the African style of living. Just a few percent of the people are wealthy. All other people are lower than the middle class or poor. Those days in the village or town, everyone knows almost everybody they love and care for each other, they share their food, no religious fight, Hindu, Muslim, Christians are studying together playing together (still this culture exists in Kerala) when Christmas comes Hindu and Muslims going their house for parties and same with Hindus and Muslim feasts and there were no boundary walls. But now most of the Keralites are middle class or wealthy (yes, a few percent of the people are still poor) all they have houses with boundary walls, and same as in Europe or America, some of the people don't know who the neighbors are. Therefore, genuine love and care are missing even within the families themselves. Like any other rich country, family members enjoy their mobile phones at home. Parents and children talking together become very limited; all have their priorities.

On my first visit to Africa in 1996, I saw my old Kerala and the honest, loving, and caring people in Africa. I visited Sudan first, then Tanzania, Kenya, Nigeria, and so on. Now some countries in Africa are better than any other countries in terms of development. I have enjoyed the African mother's care; they don't see me as if I am from another continent or country. They feel that I am one among them.

That attracted the most to go again and again to Africa. Now my friends are African more than any other nationality. After that, I visited over 37 countries, including Europe, the Middle East, the Far East, and Asia. But I like Africa better than any other country. I visit more often to Africa than any other country. Now I am doing agriculture and trading business in Africa and supplying Solar and Agricultural products. To start with a small investment Africa is the best business place. With little money in the rich country, I am still a poor man, but with the same money in developing countries like Africa, I am a wealthy man; this is my belief. This is my recommendation to the All-African Diaspora who is struggling for a job or starting a small business. Go to your motherland and start a business peacefully. You can sleep in the street. No one will question you. I don't want to say more about myself; what I recommend seeing is believing. I have described more about African History and its people in my first book, **"THE HIDDEN VOICE OF AFRICA"** please try to read it as well.

Touching Millions of hearts:

"It's more about what a man did when he was alive than how long he lived on earth."

It is written that we should do certain deeds while living on this earth. Only a few people read it and try to do those deeds. Those deeds are what are left on earth as their signature, some of which we call great or noble. Some live and die like other animals. What is the difference between them and wild animals? We become real human beings when we recognize our deeds and work for them. Only then can we see other human beings' suffering, open our minds to them, and open the door to mercy. There is no doubt that it is the black-skinned, snow-white-minded African people who deserve it the most in this age. For so long white-minded and black-minded invaders have shown no mercy to the African people or even treated them as human beings. Now God is ready to hear the prayers of those African people, and now is a good time for Africa.

Great leaders like Dr. Arikana Chihombori Quao try their best to collect one million subscribers through her organization ADDI- "The

African Diaspora Development Institute" https://ouraddi.org/ to touch the heart billion people. All African diaspora must give a hand to her to make it happen for those one million signatures to bring up an internationally recognized organization. Dr. Arikana's idea is much practical for African development. Donate One- Dollar each. It will be one million ten-dollar each 10 million, 100 dollars each 100 million. Is it impossible for the African diaspora? It's not... That fund can utilize for various development in Africa.

It is easy to sit back and commend that African leaders are corrupted, African leaders and not doing anything for Africa. Those comments are good, but what contribution will you make to Africa? When the leaders like Dr. Arikana take the pain to develop Africa, sacrificing her family time and talking continuously to the African diaspora means now you have a leader to guide you, so all African diaspora must wake up and move together with this Mama. She has a clear business plan for Africa and the African diaspora. The first step is registering your name to https://ouraddi.org/ to prove your identity and that you are an African diaspora. Let that one million numbers come first; then, it will shoot up to one billion. Once you reach that goal, no one can stop you because you become a powerful organization to demand United Nations.

Unfortunately, the present African Union's activity is not up to the mark in bringing up Africa's issues in front of the world. The first hygiene required within the African Union leadership itself. Those in the same seat for many years must surrender and give the people capable of developing Africa a chance.

No free food, no country will not do anything free for any other country. They might have seen something more significant than what they are paying if they are spending.

How many of you know about the African Union building donated by the Chinese? Here is the first mistake African leaders are accepted as a compliment.

Current tenants: Seat of the African Union in Addis Ababa, Ethiopia,

The main building was designed and built by a collaboration of Tongji University, China State Construction Engineering, and the China Architecture and Design Research Group, with the US$200 million budget donated by the Chinese government. This building was inaugurated in 2012. Of course, China will not give anything free to Africa or any other country. This is the young African descent and the African diaspora's responsibility to find the secret behind this deal. Now all young children know the microchip technology that can trace every secret. If any other country controls that building, do not expect that African Union can take any market decision within the structure.

"It is not because Africans diaspora's lack talent, courage or money but because they are not mature enough to take advantage of this opportunity"

The African diaspora must understand that Africa is rich in all prosperous such as natural resources, including agriculture. But very few present the authentic African and invested in Africa. All the investments are made by Americans, Europeans, Chinese, or Asians. It is your mistake that you are not looking into it. You are still complaining about the African leaders and the governments. In the meantime, all the business people benefit from Africa. No business in the world is without risk if you are not ready to take that risk, but others do. Be practical from now, stop complaining and come into action. Money is the primary concern in starting a business in Africa. You have to bring strategy into action then the investments will follow you from different sources if you don't have to invest. An entrepreneur does not require any money to start the business; he creates the ideas and puts the efforts into making the feasibility study, making the action plan, then presenting the company to the investors; if that is workable, investors will spend the money. Why are all Europeans, Chinese, Americans, and Asian people sharing money, investing in Africa, and minding a lot from Africa? Why can't you and your team can't do it?

Rutendo Matinyarare is an astute marketer with over 15 years of experience in various industries, including business systems, hospitality, entertainment, rubber, finance, non-profit, government, and brand management. Listen watch the YouTube videos of the young leader.

His greatest passion is to achieve marketing and branding objectives at the lowest possible cost by leveraging creativity with integrated online and offline marketing. He also has professional qualifications with PRINCE2 Project Mgt Practitioner, CIM Post Graduate, IMM. LCCI can guide you on how to the strategic business in Africa. Africa needs a leader like Rutendo Matinyarare, Joshua Maponga, and PLO Lumumba to control African Union. He is inviting all the African billionaires from the African diaspora and the Africans within Africa to join together to invest and get the benefits from Africa that others are exploiting from Africa with the use of the African Continent or its people. Yes, your only risk is spending little money on exploration.

GeoResonance company, the number one exploration company, can do that job with a very minimal amount; visit the website www. georesonance.com and contact Sebastian Joseph - Sales Manager-Middles East and Africa on email: sebastian@georesonance.co will assist you in exploring all the minerals from Africa with the full bankable feasibility study report. Their precise exploration technology can identify any minerals up to 1500 Meters deep. GeoResonance Company is willing to support the development of African Countries with no hidden agenda.

MINERAL EXPLORATION PROJECTS

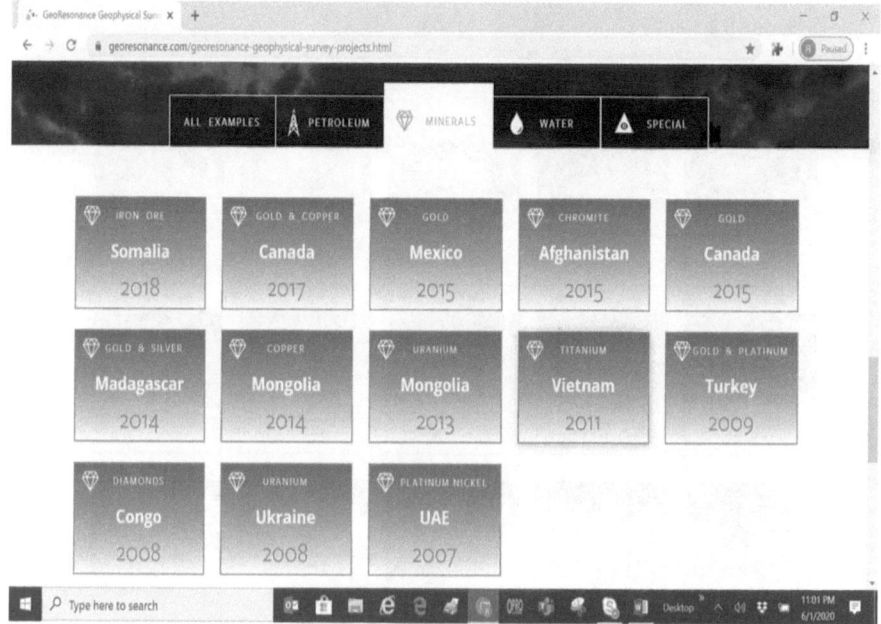

CLICK ON EACH COUNTRY ON THE WEBSITE YOU CAN SEE THE PROJECT LOCATION AND DETAILS.

OIL AND GAS EXPLORATION PROJECTS

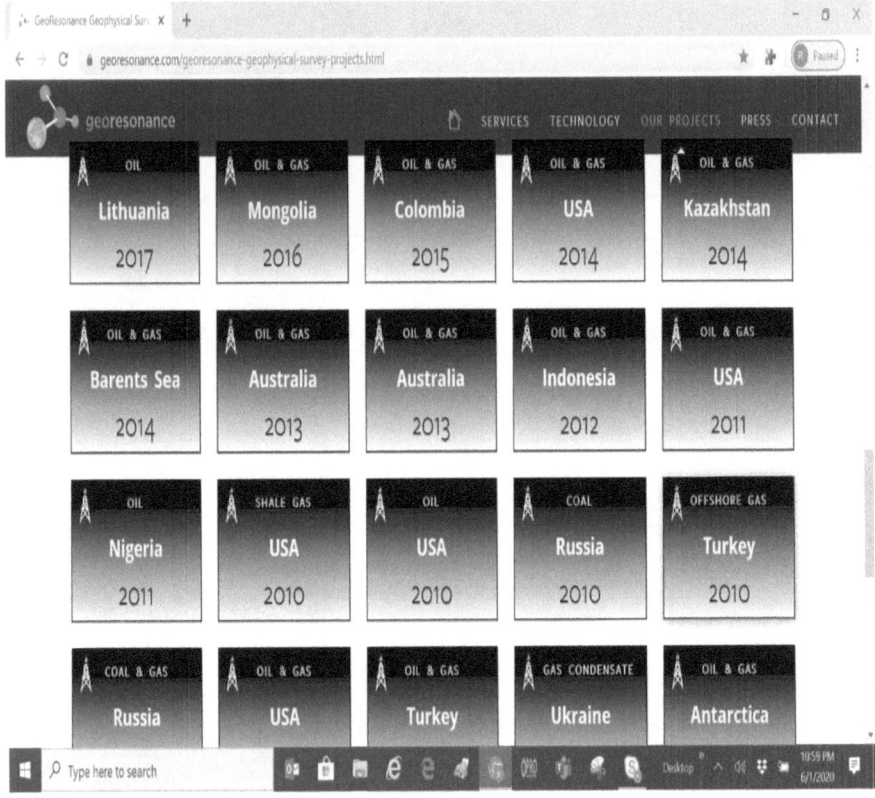

CLICK ON EACH COUNTRY ON THE WEBSITE YOU CAN SEE THE PROJECT LOCATION AND DETAILS.

The African diaspora who would like to invest in Minerals/Oil and Gas can think of associating with this company.

To the young generation of Africa and the diaspora:

"Life is like a flute. It may have many holes and emptiness, but it can play magical melodies if you work on it carefully."

It is very accurate; many people use this quote because it has much meaning and depends on how you take it. To listen to those magical melodies, you must close all the noises around you and focus only on those melodies. Otherwise, it will interrupt the rhythm of the songs.

To listen to those melodies, you must shut down your voice first and open your ears to receive those melodies so that the emptiness in your mind will be filled with peace and harmony. When your mind becomes harmonized, you will start thinking good things. Your mind is connected to the earth to control your body. Therefore, God has given to every average human being a binary system (two legs, two hands, two eyes, two years, and so on) in our body other than the tongue, and one more thing, if you don't use that correctly, you will be in trouble.

The young generation can change Africa, especially the student's union. When a country becomes operated by the colonized mentality leaders, for sure that country will never develop, and the people of that country will end up with economic crisis and poverty. It happened to many countries for generations and generations. Each time most of those countries came back to normal with the support of the student movement's revolution.

But unfortunately, it is a common practice not only in Africa but all the people around the world who are the slaves of mobile phones. A family of 3 to 5 or more members will have one or two mobiles (including me). Most of the time, this family may be sitting in one room, but no one will talk to each other. Father and mother will be talking to their friends, and the children will be chatting with their friends or playing games or other activities. No time to talk to each other within the families or not think about something better for the future, so the mobile industry conquered the early days of togetherness and love. It has become a kind of mental illness from which no one can escape. Have you noticed that when you go to a public place with many people, you can see that 90% of the people are looking at their mobiles? Thanks to mobile technology!

"When parasites spread on a tree, the tree will not be noticed at first, but when it spreads out and grows so that the tree cannot grow, it would be easily destroyed. This is because the parasites are used as food to get the tree's nutrients."

African children, this is not the time to sit back and relax because Africa is under the threat of some kind of cancer and viruses. The viruses are the European colonialists still trying to colonize Africa with the support of some existing bad leaders. Because they see the tremendous growth of Africa and some of the country's leaders' capabilities proving that Africa could build without the previous colonizers' support, including African free Trade, Africa vision 2030, Africa vision 2063, etc. But there is a limit for that leader with their capabilities. The young generation's strength is significant in terms of your intelligence and involvement in the developing activities to support the leaders. Because your present leaders and your fathers and making this vision not for them to enjoy, it is for you and your coming generations. When the 2060 vision is completed, most leaders will rest in peace in their graveyards. It is your responsibility to inherit their ideas and power from them to protect Africa from the colonizers; otherwise, their soles will never be at rest like the forefather's soles are still weeping and wailing in their graveyards.

Other cancerous viruses are in China. They are buying most of the land you should purchase for your children. They make money from your land, but you are sleeping. When the Portuguese colonized Mozambique, they did rice farming and exporting worldwide. Now Mozambique is importing rice from China. Ghana was the biggest producer of tomatoes and shipped them to Europe. Now Ghana is importing tomatoes from Italy and China with an added chemical to spoil your health. On that note, even the onion chilies are imported from China and elsewhere. What are you looking for? How much money do you need to cultivate these farms and produce agricultural products? Do not keep your brain fresh without using it.

Africa does not require any more food to import from any part of the world because Africa has everything to feed her children, but a mother can only give the rhythmic music, a lap to lay down, a heart to love, and a breeze to make you comfortable. Once you get that from your mother, you get energized and go to work and bring the food for that mother to be pleased. The Mother of Africa is giving you that abundantly, but are you doing your part to that mother?

These countries are populated mainly by the Chinese and are using the resources you are supposed to enjoy. Here we go, the number of Chinese in African countries, but most of these African Nationalities are looking the job in China or elsewhere without knowing about these opportunities in their own countries. Most Chinese invest in

Agriculture, Textile/cloth manufacturing, alcoholic drinks, Ice cream parlors, restaurants, retail shops, Road and building constructions, Mining sectors, and similar. But African diaspora is not even looking into these areas. These Chinese are using the local African people as their laborers, no graduates will be appointed to their companies in the white color jobs, and the Chinese will conquer all those jobs. Don't forget China is giving a loan to these countries and buying your land and its people, which is not a good sign for Africans.

Chinese Population over 1.6 million in African Countries until 2020. It will rise to 3 million in 2030. Does it not mean the Chinese are created 1.6 million jobs or businesses for the Chinese within Africa?

- Uganda, over 40,000
- Nigeria, over 45,000
- Kenya, over 50,000
- Angola, over 55,000
- Ethiopia, over 60,000
- Sudan, over 74,000
- Zambia, over 80,000
- Madagascar, over 100,000
- South Africa, over 400,000
- Ghana, over 700,000

Of course, to protect this many Chinese people, China needs to bring their military to Africa, so the Chinese Military is already there.

- African diaspora not coming to Africa to invest in this field; why?
- Is that you have not been aware of what is going on on the African continent?
- Or are you not smart enough like the Chinese do?
- Or are you scared of the Chinese or the African people and their leaders?

As part of Africa, 2063 schedule with 55 countries will be coming with a lot of infrastructure developments such as Airport, Seaport, Railways, Roads, Stadiums, Oil and Gas exploration, Mining,

Electricity, Water, Hotels, Schools, Colleges, etc. The opportunities never end.

Unfortunately, some of the African leaders are not good financial managers. They believe the loan offered by China and Europeans or some other nations are good for Africa but don't realize that they are surrendering their country and its people to long-term debts. This means that even the next generation yet to be born will be in debt. When they sanction loans from any source, they get some bribes that they believe are safe, but they do not know that they are preparing their graves.

Using strategic investment like some Arab countries have done during their development period would be wise. Buy for a few years, share the benefit with the investors, and after the contract period, the whole infrastructure to hand over to the same country, and the entire infrastructure will belong to the same country. It should not go beyond 20 or 25 years.

It is not the time for the African countries to cannibalize and kill each other to implement the rule of the white colonialists; instead, this is the time to understand the colonialist's bad cheating tactics and unite together; unite means One Nation, one continent, one heart, one soul, one national anthem, one military to be number one in the world which is the dream of the forefathers "The United States of Africa." If a not same word can hear again for each country, **"We today and you tomorrow,"** The Ethiopian Empire Haile Selassie said to the African leaders. They will spoil one by one country piece by piece. After that, you can see the number of countries will increase from 55 to another 55 in a few decades because the colonialist started their agenda again to colonize one by one in the form of UN sanctions or USA sanctions, etc.

Life is about a journey, but some people may miss that journey without reaching their destination. Those trying to get to that destination have some purpose; it is your mistake if you don't realize that purpose. Your forefathers had a sense they had fought for freedom from the colonialists to make you set free from slavery, and you are enjoying a better life. Now it is your responsibility to protect yourself and your generation, not to be enslaved again by the same colonialist. All the African diaspora must come to Africa to defend their motherland.

I wish as the first step of developing the United States of Africa, African Union will issue the same United States of Africa Passport to all citizens of Africa, including all diaspora around the world who wish to come back home.

IF YOU WANT TO GO FAST, GO ALONE. IF YOU WANT to GO FAR, GO TOGHER- African Proverb.

A HUMBLE REQUEST

The latest generation and the current leaders of the world are trying to make money in the easiest way possible. Nobody wants to put their hard work or effort or adequately use their brain; most of them use their shortcuts to protect themselves. The result is the current global situation with war and weapon selling. The developed countries are taking the pollution and global warming. Still, I want to ask the world leaders and the weapon suppliers who will take responsibility for the worldwide war? Who is responsible for the result of the weapons, bombs, and other artillery poised chemical exhaustion to the world? The same groups talk about global warming, pollution control, etc.; A mad President or a leader can destroy the world within a blink of an eye with the powerful nuclear weapons already stored in their military yard. More people become homeless and refugees worldwide because of war and greediness. All these are happening just because of a few global egoistic leaders. When we open any media, we see only war, death, and blood flowing on the street. The recent war with Russia, Ukraine, and NATO groups will lead to a third world war. The first and second world Wars took many lives, the same way many are dying on the street, becoming homeless, and refugees. The manufacturers want to prove that their weapons or missiles are powerful, like the children's game.

Can we get the chance to live peacefully in this world before leaving this earth?

This is a humble request to the people who are not allowed to grow Africa and forget humanity, the dictators, bad political leaders, those who wear the cover of religion, band lack, and white colonialists.

Remember: As the calf approaches its mother in the evening as thousands of cows graze together, the result of your deeds will reach you before you die. It depends on what you do to the people and the world. The next generation will probably have to suffer the consequences of those deeds that are not good.

We have seen many leaders who often forget their own country and brothers when power is in their hands, where they are today, who respect them, and perhaps many do not even like remembering their name. But some leaders have left this land with their signatures, and no matter how long it takes or how many epidemics and floods come, that signature cannot be erased.

Let me remind you of the actual incident of our beloved father of the African nation Nelson Mandela's humility, how the African people must behave toward other people when they get higher positions of power in your hand.

After becoming President, I asked some of my bodyguard members to go for a walk in town. After the hike, we went for lunch at a restaurant. We sat in one of the most central ones, and each asked what we wanted. After a bit of waiting, the waiter who brought our menus appeared; at that moment, I realized that a single man was waiting to be served at the table right in front of us.

When he was served, I told one of my soldiers: go ask that man to join us. The soldier went and transmitted my invitation. The man stood up, took the plate, and sat beside me. While eating, his hands constantly shook, and he didn't lift his head from the food. When we finished, he waved without even looking at me; I shook his hand and walked away!

The soldier said to me:

— *Madiba, that man must be very sick as his hands wouldn't stop shaking while eating.*
Not at all! The reason for his tremor is another - I replied. They looked at me weird, and I said to them:

— That man was the guardian of the jail I was locked up in. I often screamed and cried for water after the torture I was subjected to, and he came to humiliate me; he laughed at me, and instead of giving me water, he urinated on my head.

He wasn't sick; he was scared and shook, maybe fearing that I, now president of South Africa, would send him to jail and do the same thing he did with me, torturing and humiliating him. But that's not me; that behavior is not part of my character or ethics. Minds that seek revenge destroy states, while those that seek reconciliation build Nations.

We know that it is tough to change you or change yourself from the bad things that you have been doing in Africa for a long, but don't prevent the poor people's basic fundamental right of their food to fill their bellies, a shelter to sleep, and don't make the people naked in front of the world. Which will be very shameful to you as well, because since you are acting in front of these people and front of the world as you are the leaders, they are not fed by you or become naked in front of the world because of you, then to whom to be blamed? Yes, it's you only to be blamed; it will know as your incapability.

Steal what you want after fulfilling their rights because we know theft, murder, and inhumanity are your assets which no one can stop you soon. TA king in Kerala, India aid to have ruled that all human beings wanted to live happily without hunger. His name was "Mahaabali," and its festival Onam is still celebrated in Kerala for centuries. Since I was born in that country, I cannot accept that no one should live in this world without food, dress, or shelter.

Professor PLO Lumumba said in his speech that one of his wishes was that he is waiting for the day of Queen Elisabeth II of London to apologize to the world for enslaving the African people and other peoples of the world for slavery and colonization.

"If a man dies, fertilize it; we can accept it as the law of the universe, but please do not kill that man and fertilize yourself, please."

A child asked Mahatma Gandhi, "What is democracy?"

Mahatma Gandhi replied that when you win a race, democracy is not just about winning; it's also about remembering that some people ran with you.

Again, he told me that no one wins if he runs alone.

Next question to Mahatma Gandhi, "What to do with the law?"

Mahatma Gandhi replied that it must be violated, but all the crowd violence and asked him, shouldn't the law be obeyed?

He said: The law must be obeyed, and citizens must do so; until the law is fair, Justice is essential, not law.

Yes, the time has come for the African people to receive justice, and African people must wake up now................

Open the glow of love for the whole world.

May there be a new African nation (United States of Africa) in this world full of peace and happiness.